TALK OF CHAMPIONS

KENNY SMITH

TALK OF
CHAMPIONS

STORIES OF THE PEOPLE WHO MADE ME

A MEMOIR

DOUBLEDAY  NEW YORK

All rights reserved. Published in the United States by Doubleday,
a division of Penguin Random House LLC, New York, and distributed
in Canada by Penguin Random House Canada Limited, Toronto.

doubleday.com

DOUBLEDAY and the portrayal of an anchor with a dolphin are
registered trademarks of Penguin Random House LLC.

Book design by Michael Collica
Front-of-jacket photograph by Jeremy Freeman courtesy
of Warner Bros. Discovery, Inc.
Back-of-jacket photographs courtesy of the author
Jacket design by Michael J. Windsor

Library of Congress Cataloging-in-Publication Data
Names: Smith, Kenny, 1965 March 8– author.
Title: Talk of champions : stories of the people who
made me : a memoir / Kenny Smith.
Description: First edition. | New York : Doubleday, [2023]
Identifiers: LCCN 2022031281 | ISBN 9780385548052
(hardcover) | ISBN 9780385548069 (ebook)
Subjects: LCSH: Smith, Kenny, 1965 March 8– . | African American basketball
players—Biography. | Basketball players—United States—Biography. |
Sportscasters—United States—Biography. |
Basketball—United States—History—20th century.
Classification: LCC GV884.S55 A3 2023 |
DDC 796.323092 [B]—dc23/eng/20220707
LC record available at https://lccn.loc.gov/2022031281

MANUFACTURED IN THE UNITED STATES OF AMERICA
1 3 5 7 9 10 8 6 4 2
First Edition

This book is dedicated to my family.

*First, to my mom and dad—thank you for believing
in me, which made me believe in myself.*

*Thank you to my sisters, Wanda and Gwendolyn,
and my brother, Vincent, who at times sacrificed their
dreams for me to live my dreams in real time.*

*And thank you to my children, Kayla, KJ, Monique,
Malloy, and London, who actually inspire me
and show me every day that my dreams are futile
in the face of the plan God has in store.*

CONTENTS

TALK OF CHAMPIONS

"I HAD TO JOIN THE MARCH"

Sitting in my chair on the TNT set between Charles Barkley and Ernie Johnson, my head was swimming with confusion over what to do next.

This was August 28, 2020, and the Milwaukee Bucks had just walked off the court before a playoff game in protest of yet another police shooting of an unarmed Black man.

It didn't feel right to me to be on the air with all this going on, but there I was: the cameras were rolling, the producers were counting down, and Ernie, our host, was about to begin.

Ernie typically looks around at the start of the show to see which of the panelists—me, Charles, or Shaquille O'Neal—he wants to go to first. This time he glanced at me. Seeing that I was lost in my thoughts and not ready to talk, he tossed to Charles instead.

I don't even know what Charles said, because I might as well have been in space. When Ernie turned to me a second time, I still wasn't sure exactly what I was going to do.

"Kenny?" he said.

I shook my head, scratched my face, and shuffled in my chair.

"This is tough," I finally said. After talking for a few moments, trying to express the conflict churning inside me, I got to the point.

"As a Black man and former player," I said, "I think it's best for me to support the players and just not be here tonight."

I unplugged my microphone and earpiece, stood from my chair, and walked off the set.

"I respect that," Ernie said.

Charles was quiet. I would later find out that he was angry with me. That's OK, too. What I did had nothing to do with him. It was the culmination of a crazy year of turmoil in the country and of reflection for me.

As we were already dealing with a global pandemic, the spring and summer of 2020 brought new incidents of police brutality and racial injustice. Video of those terrible events spread across social media. All over the country, activists and regular citizens took to the streets in protest.

Between that and all the time I spent at home reflecting and reconnecting, something in me had shifted.

I just couldn't sit there on the TNT set and be a talking head. I had to join the march.

.   .   .

These memoirs are a blueprint of the lessons derived from my intimate relationships with the greatest of greats, from Michael Jordan to Dean Smith to Hakeem Olajuwon to Bill Russell to Shaquille O'Neal to so many others. I am a product of the people who formed me, and now I want to share their wisdom.

Above all else, this book is for you—my kids. I'm talking straight to you, Kayla Brianna, KJ, Monique, Malloy, and London. We had quite a year together in 2020: hanging out and thinking deeply on where our lives were going in ways that changed and impacted us in 2021, 2022, and beyond.

But this book is also for anyone who wants to follow along as if you are one of my family members. I'm sure that the COVID-19 pandemic caused many people to think about their own lives, just as we did at our house.

I've learned a lot of hard lessons over my fifty-eight years and experienced my share of triumphs, too. It all led me to that moment of increased consciousness, and I want to retrace that path for you.

I've had the opportunity to play with Michael Jordan at the University of North Carolina at Chapel Hill, and for the legendary UNC coach Dean Smith. To win NBA championships alongside Hakeem Olajuwon in Houston. To help launch an Emmy-winning broadcast, then take it to new heights with my current partners Ernie, Charles, and Shaq.

The way I look at it, it would be selfish to hold to myself all the information that I've been fortunate enough to acquire. This book is my small contribution to an era of awakening and action.

Before the pandemic hit, I told you all that 2020 would be "harvest season" for you. I put that on every hashtag on social media and every text I sent you that year as the final message: #HarvestSeason.

I talked to you all about planting the seeds of hard work and how this would be the year to harvest the fruit of your labor. And 2020 started with that happening.

Kayla Brianna: At twenty-six, you had settled into your new apartment across town and continued to blossom as an actress and singer.

Monique: At twenty-three, you had just recently moved out of the guesthouse (I cried upon realizing that my first batch of kids was out of the nest) and got your own apartment across the street from your sister. Then you landed a starring role as a series regular on a new TV sitcom.

KJ: At twenty-two, you were finishing your junior year at the University of North Carolina. You had gone from a walk-on player to earning a scholarship at one of the most prestigious academic and basketball institutions in the country. Add to that the fact that you were in the starting five for several games and played major minutes in key situations. Impressive—but still not as impressive as the life you've begun since.

Malloy: At twelve, you were about to graduate from elementary school and excited about your new challenges in middle school—and you were accepted to every middle school to which you applied.

London: Honestly, I don't typically compare the five of you children, but at seven you have the best qualities of all the siblings rolled into one, so look out, world! And you're still so young!

The curse of the pandemic did bring a silver lining for our family. Under no other circumstances would I have had all of you back in the house at one time, a blended family together again.

I'm happy that you older children decided to spend a large amount of lockdown with me. None of us expected the pandemic to go multiple months before the return of any normalcy, let alone stretch into the next few years. But our open conversations during those initial months—over dinner, game nights, TikTok videos, and movie nights—are moments that I will remember forever. The honesty of our conversations—conversations about love, fear, anger, aspirations, and many other topics that meant so much to us—was transformational for me as a father.

Through this memoir, I want those conversations to continue. The worst of the pandemic seems over, and we haven't been in lockdown together for some time now. But the experiences of 2020 and 2021 changed us forever, forcing us to look inward and lean on those closest to us for new levels of support.

Of course, it wasn't just our lives that came to a screeching halt when the pandemic hit. The world of major sports also stopped. After an extended shutdown, the NBA created an environment in Orlando, Florida, to enable the resumption of a shortened season. All players, coaches, and staff going into the "bubble" at Walt Disney World were tested frequently for the coronavirus. For the first forty-five days, no guests were allowed. Players and staff who elected to leave were subject to a ten-day quarantine upon re-entry.

Months earlier, I had created a similar bubble for our home. No in and outs, no visitors. I wanted a safe, secure, and healthy environment. You guys laughed as I disinfected your clothes after you came inside—from hanging out in the backyard.

OK, I may have overdone it. Ha-ha.

Everyone around the world was forced to stay home. No work, no play, nothing extracurricular. The pandemic showed families around the world what they had built over the years. We had no choice but to confront questions we might have avoided during busier times:

Can we live in what we built?
Are we happy with it?
What needs fixing?
What needs to be painted, externally and internally?

And even more to the point, who are we?

I started with traditional home repair, fixing leaky faucets, tightening chairs, and touching up paint on the walls. It then went to fixing windows and redecorating rooms. I would move a picture, change the angle of the couch, put a rug in one room instead of another.

After all the DIY projects stopped, it was time for the real touch-ups and repairs—the minds and bodies of the people inside our home, and our relationships.

I asked myself, *What needs to be repaired?* And, even more to the point, *Who am I?* We asked one another in the family, *Who are you?*

The answers to those essential questions are the keys to becoming a champion at whatever we do. We have to know ourselves. In sports, every championship team has an identity, a style of play. Are you a team that plays up-tempo like the Golden State Warriors with Steph Curry and Klay Thompson? They move fast and their goal is to get the first available good shot early on the shot clock. Everyone who plays against them has to be ready for the speed.

Do you play through a specific person like the Lakers do with LeBron James, where one player has the ball the majority of the time while others read and react off his movements? Are you a defensive-minded team? Keep the score low and hope that you have the ability to score and stop opponents in key possessions?

Style of play is the first component that establishes who you are. Identity allows you to develop players, make trades, and add free agents to your team.

To my kids I say, Now apply that same mentality to you as a person. What areas do you need to develop? What areas do you need to trade for or acquire? What person or thing do you need to add to your life?

The year 2020 also reminded me of the mantra at my high school, Archbishop Molloy (whom you're named after, Malloy): "*Non scholae sed vitae,*" which is Latin for "Not for school but for life."

This is the story of how people shaped me—and prepared me for the unique moment we faced in 2020 and will continue to face beyond.

.   .   .

Back to the moment when I was sitting on the set at TNT.

I hadn't watched the Jacob Blake video at first. Why did I need to see another slave movie? I've seen *Roots.* I've seen *12 Years a Slave.* Why did I need to see another Black person get shot?

But after a few days I finally broke down and checked out for myself the footage that had gone viral on social media. It showed a police officer in Kenosha, Wisconsin, opening fire on an unarmed Black man as he began to get into an SUV in which his three children sat.

Unfortunately, I wasn't surprised. Growing up in the inner city, I've seen people being grabbed up by police. I haven't seen it escalate to a shooting, but I've seen how it can get there.

Reflecting on the incident and the viral video of it, I was most sensitive to what it meant for you kids, especially the older ones. I noticed that this, along with the deaths of George Floyd and Breonna Taylor, was the first time racial violence and injustice touched your generation that hard and for that long.

As this was all going on, I was traveling back and forth between our home in Los Angeles and Atlanta, where we shot our TNT show, *Inside the NBA*.

On August 27, I heard rumblings that the Milwaukee Bucks, who in a non-pandemic year play their games a mere forty-five minutes from where the officer shot Jacob Blake, might stage some kind of protest.

I wasn't surprised to hear that players could take action. Some in the NBA, like Kyrie Irving of the Brooklyn Nets, had already expressed concerns about participating in the bubble, because there were so many important things going on outside the world of sports.

Don't underestimate how disconnected the players thought they were from what was happening in the streets. The guys I talked to had a sense of isolation.

They felt like, *Man, we're playing games and we're not doing anything, and everybody's out there suffering.*

When the Blake shooting happened, I think everyone in the bubble was just spent. I understand that they felt their voices weren't being heard, even though it was the exact opposite. When the games began, the phrase "Black Lives Matter" was painted on the courts. The players had messages demanding social justice stitched onto the backs of their jerseys. In postgame interviews, they raised important issues.

It was all being heard around the world. It was aiding the cause. It was just hard for the players themselves to see that from inside the bubble. After the Bucks walked off, the NBA canceled the remainder of its games for the night.

I was in Atlanta getting ready for a pregame show. My first thought was, *I guess I'm going home to LA today. Why would I stay around here when there are no games?*

Then one of our TNT producers emailed. The network wanted us to do an hour-long show. That surprised me. If there weren't any games, what would we talk about?

Keeping an open mind, I emailed back.

"OK," I wrote. "What's the format?"

The network wanted our perspective on the Bucks walking off. Should they forfeit the game? How would it impact the series?

That was totally understandable, but it wasn't the perspective that I was looking for. The appropriate perspective to me was, what is the state of the world? My mind was far from the implications of the protest on basketball.

So when I heard the plan for the show, it's not that it rubbed me the wrong way, but it did get my antennas up. It alerted me that not everyone was seeing this issue the way I was seeing it. Getting ready for work, I was wrestling with it. *We're really going to talk about basketball?*

I suggested doing a whole hour strictly on social injustice. The producers assured me that our show would be very heavy with those issues. I agreed to come in but couldn't shake the idea that it didn't feel right.

I called KJ. "I'm thinking about being silent for a segment," I said, interested in gauging his reaction. "When Ernie asks me something, I'll just be like, 'You know, Ernie, I'm just gonna be quiet.'"

"Yeah, I don't know . . . ," KJ said. We both agreed that I should do something but hadn't quite hit on the right approach.

We kicked some ideas back and forth and said good-bye. I arrived at the station at six forty-five for a seven p.m. show. During normal times, we get there much earlier to dress and visit the makeup room, but the pandemic disrupted that routine. Now we would just show up, powder our faces, and begin.

When I got there, the doors opened the same as always. The security guard was the same. Inside, everyone was in production mode—the cameramen, the crew, the producers. Which they should have been. That was their job. They were supposed to be ready to work.

But it hit me hard to see the world going on as if nothing had happened.

Everything's the same, I thought, looking around the set. The phrase kept repeating in my head, along with another one: *Nothing has changed.*

Nothing has changed. Everything's the same.

Right then I knew that this was not going to work.

I called KJ again.

"I'm not gonna be there," I said.

"What do you mean?"

"I'm not gonna stay," I said. "I'm just going home."

"Are you gonna go home now?"

"No, because then it would look like I stormed off or something. I think I have to go on and then not be a part of it."

"How you gonna do it?"

"I don't know, but it doesn't feel right. It just does not feel right."

"If it don't feel right, Daddy, then don't do it."

When I sat at the desk, it was more of that uneasy feeling.

The sound guy put on my mic, like he always did. Ernie was in the same chair as always, as were Charles, Shaq, and me.

Nothing has changed. Everything's the same.

Ernie started the show: five, four, three, two, one. . . . I was like, *This ain't right, man, this ain't right. This guy just got shot seven times. Broad daylight.*

When Ernie asked me to speak, I stood and walked off. On my way off the set, it didn't cross my mind what the producers were thinking, what my castmates were thinking, what the people at home were thinking.

My only thought was: *Shit should not be the same.*

Back in my dressing room, I regained a bit of composure and began to form a plan for what came next.

Because I hadn't told anyone beforehand what I was going to do, I decided to wait around until the end of the show to talk to Charles, Shaq, and Ernie. I wanted to tell them that it had been a largely spontaneous gesture, not intended to put them in a bad position.

While waiting, I heard a knock at the door. It was a member of the crew, a Black man with whom I chatted all the time.

"That was real," he said, quivering with emotion.

That was it for me. I lost it. Bawling.

Why am I crying? I thought. *What am I crying for?*

It was the emotion of what we were feeling as a culture. It was all just so raw.

My phone rang. It was KJ.

"You all right?" he said.

I pulled myself together and told him that I was.

"Man, that was powerful," he told me.

Then I called my daughters. After that my phone just started going bonkers. Radio stations, friends—anyone who knew how to catch me was calling. I didn't want to make this a media event. I know that sounds strange because, well, of course it was a media event. But this wasn't supposed to be about me. I turned my phone off.

Then I decided to go home. There was an eight forty-five p.m. Delta flight to LA, and I bought a ticket. Then I grabbed my bag and started packing.

The show ended. Charles, Ernie, and Shaq walked off the set and toward the dressing rooms.

Shaq came first. He's an interesting guy—he's with you, but he's not gonna be the one who talks to you emotionally in the moment. Later on, he's like a big teddy bear. But in the moment he plays it cool.

"Yo, man, I just want you to know, I did that in the moment," I said. "I didn't know I was going to do it. I don't want you to feel like I put you in a bad spot."

"Nah, nah, that's you," Shaq said. "It's cool."

Charles just kind of nodded. He didn't really respond. And then Ernie stopped.

"I really respect what you did, and I get where you're coming from," he said.

Tim Kiely, our producer, came running down the hall, all excited. Tim and I have an honest relationship. We tell it like it is. He'll be like, "You were terrible today," and I'll respond, "No, you were terrible." But we love each other. He's always been in my corner.

"You're the fucking greatest, Kenny!" he shouted. "That's why you're here. No one would have had the balls to do what you just did. Man, that's what makes you you. That's what America needed to see." I was glad he understood what the moment meant to me, because TK is someone I respect. And as he isn't African American, I felt proud that my message had come across.

I left for the airport, which is only fifteen minutes from the studio. This was the first time I had flown commercial since the pandemic began; I was so scared of COVID that I'd been paying for private flights between LA and Atlanta.

At the airport I was masked up and wearing a hoodie as I went through security. Thinking that would make me unrecognizable, I was surprised to hear the shout-outs.

"Smith, man, that was real what you did!" one of the TSA agents said. Others jumped in with similar compliments, as did folks in the line.

By the time I got on the plane, I was completely exhausted. I collapsed into my seat and fell asleep for the duration of the flight.

Upon landing, I finally turned on my phone and was greeted by roughly three hundred texts and another three hundred emails. There were messages from radio and TV stations everywhere, plus nephews, cousins, seemingly everyone I'd ever met.

Before doing anything else, I FaceTimed Malloy. He doesn't always watch the show, so I didn't know how aware he was of what had happened.

When he picked up he started clapping.

"Dad," he said. "That was big."

"Man, I didn't know if you would get it, Malloy."

"I got it. My friends were like, 'Your dad understands what's going on in the culture.'"

It meant so much to me that the moment had resonated with Malloy. We said good night, and the day was finally over.

.   .   .

There was one wrinkle left. Not long after, Charles was doing a podcast interview with the former NBA star Vince Carter and was asked about my walkout.

"I was pissed at Kenny," Charles said. "Because I didn't think he should have walked off. He should have told us in advance . . . I had no problem with him walking off. He should have told us so we could have prepared. The show was like, 'Uh-oh.' "

Let me back up for a second and talk about Charles.

My relationship with him is, I don't like him. I love him. He's a brother. I love him almost the same way I love my biological brother.

Without Charles Barkley, I wouldn't have had the platform to do what I did. He brought social and political consciousness and pop culture to TNT. Before he joined, we were a funny, informative basketball show. Charles made us a TV show. He gave me the courage to talk about anything.

A lot of times, his views on social issues are different from mine. They're not always radically different, but sometimes they are.

One point that we disagreed on was when Charles said the Milwaukee Bucks should have alerted their opponent about their protest. You don't alert people when you see social injustice. You just do what you have to do. It's supposed to be disruptive.

The only unfair bit of what Charles did on the podcast was when he failed to mention that I had waited for him to come off the set. His comment could have been, "Yeah, I was pissed when he did it, but Kenny did wait until the end of the show and had that conversation with me."

That was the part that was a little bit sketchy to me. But maybe he didn't remember it because it was all happening so fast.

Look, Charles is a walking contradiction, but he's my walking contradiction. At times people are like, "Charles is an Uncle Tom."

And then Charles will give a million dollars to Morehouse College. Or he'll go make a speech at Alabama State. Then he'll say something that contradicts everything that he has just done for Black colleges.

We all have people like that, people whom we love who contradict who they are at times. We've all got uncles like that. Charles is the uncle at the cookout. You have to love him though, because every now and then you're like, "Uncle made sense today."

Immediately after that podcast came out, people were saying, "Are you going to go back at him? Are you gonna debate it on TV?"

For me to do that, to go after another Black man, and one who I call my brother—that would not have been Black excellence. That would have been divisive. And that's what "the man" or "the system" wants. It wants to pit us against people who are like-minded or who are otherwise with us. It wants to divide and conquer, and I was not going to do that.

And after all, what is any of this about—the lessons of the pandemic, the introspection, the time reconnecting, the consciousness-raising tragedies of George Floyd, Breonna Taylor, and Jacob Blake—if it doesn't show us a way to be our better selves?

That's what this book is all about. The people and experiences who made me think, made me who I am, made me want to be better.

For the rest of the story, I'm going to write to the entire audience, rather than directly to you kids. This book is not only for you; it's also for everyone who can relate to our experiences during these crazy, unstable few years in the country and world.

But please know that the reason I'm doing this in the first place—the reason I do anything, really—is because I want to share what's important to me with you.

CHAPTER ONE

MICHAEL JORDAN

EYE OF THE TIGER

I was jealous of Scottie Pippen. All through our playing days, and even today—I'm still jealous of Scottie Pippen.

The Chicago Bulls were considering choosing me. Their front office brought me in beforehand and asked about Michael Jordan, my old teammate at the University of North Carolina.

"He gets on guys," they said. "He won't pass the ball. He'll scream at his teammates in practice. How would you handle that?"

The question seemed silly. Why would anyone have a problem learning from Michael, no matter how he delivered feedback? Plus, he only got on the guys who needed it. That wasn't me.

"He wouldn't do that to me," I said. "Because he knows I can play."

They looked at me kind of funny. Soon after, the Bulls chose Scottie. I went to the Sacramento Kings with the very next pick.

In that moment and for many years after, I couldn't shake the feeling that Michael would have helped me become a perennial All-Star, even a Hall of Famer. His competitiveness would have taken me to another level.

I watched Scottie mature into that, and I felt it could have been me, because I know what type of energy Michael brings into you if you're open to it. I watched Steve Kerr and B. J. Armstrong play alongside Michael and I thought, *I don't know if they understand what he's bringing to them.*

During the quarantine period of 2020, when the Jordan documentary *The Last Dance* was all the sports world could talk about, I laughed at the guys who said they didn't like it when Michael got on them in practice.

If you connect with what Michael is really about, you realize that he's actually generous. He's going to share what makes him great and allow that once-in-a-lifetime competitive spirit to rub off on you.

In *The Last Dance,* they showed the famous image of Michael hugging the NBA championship trophy and crying after he won his first title in 1991.

Most people thought he was crying because he won. But that wasn't it. He cried because he competed and left it all out there. It was the release of all that competitive energy that made him emotional. He would have cried the same way if he'd lost.

How do I know this? At North Carolina, juniors and seniors had to share a room on the road with freshmen and sophomores. Often as an underclassman I would room with Michael, who was two years ahead of me.

When you're eighteen or nineteen years old, you have conversations that you don't have at thirty. You're still vulnerable and figuring out who you are. This is when he was Mike Jordan, a kid from the South who wore corny clothes and drove a corny car. A kid who liked a girl at school who didn't really like him back. He wasn't yet Michael Jordan, American icon.

We'd be lying there in the dark, trying to sleep after a game, well past midnight.

"Smith? You awake?" he'd say from across the room.

"Yeah, I'm awake."

And we'd spend the next few hours talking about our dreams and fears, developing a bond that would survive through later decades in which we hardly saw each other.

. . .

The school bell rang at 2:20 p.m., signaling the end of the day at Archbishop Molloy High School in Queens, New York. It was 1981 and I was in the eleventh grade.

Desks slid across the floor and lockers slammed. My two best friends and teammates, George Kingland and Chris Sterling, and I dashed out of the school. There was no basketball practice that day, and for kids our age that represented a special few hours of freedom.

If you skipped every other stair as you sprinted out of the building, you could catch the N train that pulled in at two thirty and be home by three. It wasn't that there was anything particularly exciting waiting for us at home; it's more that teenagers are in a hurry to get as far from school as they can, as quickly as possible.

Archbishop Molloy was an all-boys school at the time, and the sheer energy and testosterone pouring out of that building every afternoon must have been something to behold. This was a Friday, which brought the frenzy up yet another notch.

We busted out of the school and ran the 334 yards to the Main Street subway station (yes, we had measured it).

As we rushed down the subway steps, we could hear the train pull into the station. Chris, George, and I ripped off our parochial school–mandated neckties, because we didn't want to be seen in them by either a cute girl or a tough guy who might want to make a victim of a private school kid.

We dropped our tokens in the slot and ran through the turnstile as we heard the automated voice saying, "The doors are now closing."

We slithered through the doors as they sealed off the kids on the platform who hadn't quite made it. We turned and laughed at them.

Breathing as if we'd just run wind sprints after practice, we collapsed onto the plastic seats—and that's when I heard the crackle and pop. It sounded like I'd sat on a bag of potato chips.

My first thought was to look behind me to see if there was indeed something on the seat, so I tried to stand. I couldn't. My knee had gone extremely wrong, and I couldn't even straighten my leg.

By the end of the day I learned that my growth plate had broken off and was dislodged inside the joint of my knee. The doctors said surgery was necessary, and just like that all my dreams fell into serious jeopardy. Playing on national television, advancing to college and the NBA—it was all endangered.

When I woke from the surgery, the concern on my face must have been obvious. My dad, standing next to my mom at the side of the bed, saw it and made a perfectly timed comment that reignited the drive in me.

"This injury can stop you and you can become a lamb," he said. "Or you can work hard to become a tiger. Who's eating who?"

I decided to work. I decided to be a tiger.

Over the next six months my brother Vince, a basketball savant, devised a custom practice routine that I could handle while rehabbing the knee.

Me, Vince, and my dad ran six miles together every day. We came up with drills: dribbling a basketball up the stairs, dribbling two basketballs as we evaded a dodgeball, shooting over my brother as he held a broom trying to swat our shots.

Within six months I had not only worked my way back from the injury but had gone from having no scholarship offers to being recruited by nearly every school in the country.

A first-team All-American, I narrowed my choices to Duke University, the University of Virginia, and the University of North Carolina. UNC was my final visit of the three.

The legendary coach Dean Smith came to New York to watch

me score 41 points against Bishop Loughlin Memorial High School and its star point guard Mark Jackson, who later became an NBA All-Star, head coach, and ABC/ESPN analyst. Mark dropped 39 that night, but we came out on top.

Coach Smith and I then flew down to Chapel Hill together. When I arrived on campus, he assigned two players to chauffeur me around, Buzz Peterson and a sophomore who, a year earlier, had hit the game winner against Georgetown University to capture a national championship. His name was Michael Jordan.

That day I met Mike, not Michael. To a New Yorker like me, he seemed very southern. I was used to seeing colored jeans or gabardine pants, Kangol hats, and Adidas. Mike wore skinny jeans, a light blue tennis shirt, and Converse sneakers.

In New York, style ruled, and hip-hop ruled. Mike listened to R&B and didn't even know about rap music.

He was not actually a big shot at school that year. Sam Perkins was a four-time first-team All-American, and he ruled the campus. But as great as Sam was, I sensed pretty quickly that Michael had a certain "it" factor—not a skill set, but a mindset.

It started with an ability to be confident but inclusive, aggressive but caring. As he and Buzz showed me around campus, I came down with the flu, with symptoms that worsened as the day went on.

"Can you guys take me back to my room?" I asked.

Mike looked at Buzz.

"Let's stop by the pharmacy and get city boy some flu medicine," he said.

This might have been nothing more than a tossed-off comment to him, but it was my first experience with anyone in my male peer group outwardly showing concern.

In New York we had to fend for ourselves. A friend might have said, "Bro, you better think about getting some meds in you."

That difference, subtle but meaningful, was cool to me.

"Hey, Mr. New York," Mike added. "Don't worry, I get a lot of players sick when they come through Chapel Hill."

That brought out my New York competitiveness, and I got a little defensive.

"I'm not sick," I said. "My game is sick, sick as in lethal."

Mike turned to Buzz. Both were smiling.

"We have a real one here!" Mike said. "I like him!"

That evening I went back to my room for a nap. Feeling feverish, I slept through a dinner that the team had planned for me. At one point I felt someone shaking my shoulder; looking up, I saw Mike and Buzz standing over me, checking to make sure I was OK.

By the morning my fever broke and I joined the team at practice.

"Hey, New York, watch this!" Mike yelled as I walked into the gym. "Class is in session!"

That would prove to be one of his favorite lines, and I always loved it. Basketball is a thinking man's game, a school with different subjects.

This practice was a master class. Mike had an unparalleled understanding of the game. *Look at this country bumpkin thinking ahead of everyone else,* I thought. His skill set, however, didn't yet match his intellect. I rated him a B plus. His jump shot and his ball handling needed improvement.

This practice was also the first time I had seen so many seven-footers on one team: Sam Perkins. Warren Martin. Brad Daugherty. Their size intimidated me.

I can't play here, I thought. *I'm not good enough.*

This was the first time in my life I'd looked at other players and felt they were simply better. Even on other college visits I hadn't experienced this. At that moment I knew I couldn't go to the University of North Carolina. I was scared in the same way as after my knee surgery.

Practice ended and Mike called out to me.

"Hey, city boy," he said. "We'll be out in a second. We'll take you to get something to eat."

Mike strutted to his blue Monte Carlo, which he had just gotten and was so proud of. Being from New York, the car was corny as hell to me—an old man car. But it was clean and new and I didn't have a car at all, so I just laughed to myself.

We jumped in. I was quiet. Mike blasted his music as we drove to the restaurant. More R&B.

"What do you think, New York?" Mike said. "You think you're coming here?"

"I'm not sure," I said. "I got to think about it."

We stopped at a traffic light. He turned to me.

"You're coming," he said. "You know why?"

I looked back at him but said nothing.

"You got that eye," he said. "That eye like I have. It's the eye of the tiger."

Then, I kid you not, he popped a cassette into the tape deck. "Eye of the Tiger," that song from *Rocky III*, started blasting. We laughed and sang along.

I thought back to a year earlier, when I woke up from surgery and my dad asked if I was a lamb or a tiger. After the knee injury, I'd chosen to run toward what scared me, not away from it.

Though I didn't announce it until a month later, I decided at that moment to join Mike and play at UNC.

. . .

Mike and I got along great the whole year we played together. It was always, "Kenny, you're going to New York—here's two hundred dollars. Can you buy me that belt and hat you've got?"

He was country and I had all the New York gear. At that time, if you went looking for a pair of Adidas in North Carolina, they only came in one color. In New York, I could get them in orange, blue, almost any color.

"How do you get orange Adidas?" he would say.

"Man, it's right around the corner. I'll get you some."

That stuff was fun, but it was on the court that he really changed my life. Michael forces you to reach in for your greatness. Some people can find it on their own. Some just don't have it. And some people need to be around someone who can help them bring it out. That was me.

At UNC, Coach Smith created a family atmosphere that was unique at the time. Pros would come back on campus in the fall, and it was like Thanksgiving, getting people back together.

You would see twenty pros walking around. You're going to class and all of a sudden Al Wood of the Atlanta Hawks drives up and says, "Young fella, you need a ride to class?" As a freshman you could easily get starstruck.

We would also scrimmage in the gym, us versus the pros. My freshman year, Sam Perkins was a senior and Michael was a junior, so they got to be captains. I hadn't been playing much, so I was shocked when Michael started by saying, "Smith." I was the first pick.

Oh shit, I thought. I knew he saw something in me, but this was a major endorsement.

"Look," Michael told me after I jogged over to him. "If we lose, we're not getting back on the court with all these pros in the gym. So we ain't losing today. I'm picking you because we ain't losing."

I looked around the gym. There was Walter Davis, who played for Phoenix. Phil Ford of the Kansas City Kings (now the Sacramento Kings). Mitch Kupchak from the Lakers. Al Wood.

And Michael thought I gave him the best chance to win? He was pushing all the right buttons to get me motivated.

Once we started playing, Michael was talking to the pros like they were high schoolers.

"Walter can't guard me on that side," he yelled. "Throw it over to this side. I'm coming out, Kenny, I'm coming out."

I'm thinking, *That's Walter Davis, the three-time, four-time All-Star. You're in college and you're talking to him like that?* I would have laughed, but the game was too intense. In fact, Michael was single-handedly turning a normal pickup game into the NCAA finals. He brought that out of not only himself and his teammates, but also the opponent.

These NBA guys, who must have started out assuming they were going to win easily, were suddenly calling huddles to draw up plays. There's Kupchak, Davis, the whole group scrambling to figure out how to beat us.

It didn't work. We won the first game. I went to get a drink of water and returned to see Michael still standing at center court.

"I want all of them to know," he said. "I want Walter, I want Al—I want all of them to know that I'm gonna be the last man standing, and I don't need water. I'm gonna be right here."

"OK," I said. "After we win I'm not getting water either. I'm standing here with you."

We won again and then remained together in the middle of the court.

"Who's next?" Michael said. "Who's gonna stay on? Who isn't getting water?"

There was something different about this guy. What I see with great players who came after Michael, like Kobe, LeBron, Kevin Durant, Kyrie Irving—from a distance, they don't always seem to share that thought process. Michael always shared. He was happy if you came along.

Now, if you said, "No, I'm not doing it," then he had an issue with you. But he would share that IT. Whatever that IT was—

and it's hard to define or put into words—he'd share it. He'd be like, *Yo, this is IT. This is what makes it IT. You can come along with me.*

Another time that fall, he didn't pick me for his team during a scrimmage that didn't include the pros. As we started playing I said, "I want Mike. I want to guard Mike."

He looked at me. "Oh, you want to guard me?"

"Yeah, because you can't go left," I said. "Your handle is shaky."

"Oh, my handle is shaky?"

This was New York psychology. I was saying this to help him, not just talk trash. I knew he was going to work on that after hearing it from me.

Now fast-forward a year. Mike was a rookie in the NBA and came back for the pickup games in September.

"I got Mike," I said.

We started playing, and his ball handling was much improved over the previous fall.

"Oh," he said. "My handle ain't shaky now, right?"

I smiled. But inside I thought, *Oh shit, he remembered.*

That wasn't the only time he amazed me by the way he handled constructive criticism. Just like I used to tell him his handle was weak, I would say, "I don't understand how you miss jump shots. Your form is perfect. I miss sometimes because my form isn't perfect, but I don't know how you miss."

"Oh, OK," he said, very matter-of-fact and confident. "Well, I ain't gonna miss none anymore."

"What do you mean you ain't gonna miss none?" I said.

Who thinks like that? But that's the level of intensity with Michael Jordan.

It wasn't just on the court either. Once at school, when Mike was already in the NBA, he had come back with boxes of Nike Air Jordan stuff and was passing it out.

Joking around, I quoted the Run-DMC line, "Calvin Klein's no friend of mine / Don't want nobody's name on my behind," but changed it to, "Michael Jordan is a friend of mine / But I don't wear nobody's name on my behind."

He just said, "All right, Smith."

For the rest of our time in school, all the other guys regularly received boxes of shoes and clothes. How much Air Jordan stuff have I gotten from Michael in my life? None. He remembers everything.

When I got to the Sacramento Kings my rookie season, my back-court partner was Reggie Theus. Reggie was a six-foot-seven point guard and a really good player—even a great player at times.

He had been with the Chicago Bulls for six years, but they traded him in 1984, the same year they drafted Michael. Reggie then made some comments to people that the Bulls had made a mistake and that no rookie could do what he did.

The night before we played the Bulls for the first time in my rookie season, a mutual friend of Michael's and mine told me to come down to the hotel to hang out with them.

Michael was sitting with a group of guys in the room playing cards and smoking a cigar. He had both private security and Bulls' security around him; it felt like I was in the presence of a celebrity in a way that I hadn't felt before.

Sure, I'd seen Michael the past few years when he came back to UNC for the pickup games, but that was in Chapel Hill, where it felt like old times.

Now I was a bit uncomfortable, because I didn't want him to think I was there as a hanger-on, wanting to be part of his scene because he had gotten so big.

But when he looked up, he smiled.

"Oh, Kenny, waddup!" he said.

"Hey, what's good."

The very next thing he did after that greeting was pull the cigar out of his mouth, look right at me, and say, "You tell that damn Reggie Theus I didn't forget what he said, and tell him I'm gonna give him fifty tomorrow. Fifty."

That brought out the New Yorker in me.

"You ain't gonna do nothing," I said, starting in on why the individual players on my team matched up favorably against the Bulls.

Michael narrowed his eyes.

"Are you serious?" he said. "All those dudes are scared of me."

I didn't know the league yet. I didn't know the fear he put in guys. In my mind he was still Mike Jordan, the dude who drove a corny car and was desperate for orange Adidas. The dude whose handle was a little suspect. He was not Michael Jordan to me yet.

The next day at shootaround, I was running my mouth to Reggie like the New York rookie that I was.

"Reg, I was over with Mike last night and he said he was gonna give you fifty and gonna bust your ass! And I was like, 'No you're not.'"

Reggie surprised me when he didn't find it amusing at all. In fact, he was mad at me.

"Why you doing that?" he said. "Why you starting that up?"

I was beginning to see the effect that Michael had on other players.

Reggie was typically an extremely confident guy. He looked like a model. Women swooned over him. We used to joke that when Reggie walked into a room, the room would tilt because all the women went to his side. And now he was shaken up just because I might have stirred up Michael?

We won the game by 2 points and Michael scored 37. Afterward I was getting dressed and trying to get to the bus. Michael opened the door to our locker room, crossing a line that is almost never crossed.

"Theus!" he yelled. "I only had thirty-seven tonight. I told Kenny I was gonna get your ass fifty. But we in Chicago soon, I'll see you there."

In that twenty-four-hour period, Michael had shown me what the league was all about: confidence. Everyone has the skills. The trick is to take someone else's confidence.

Michael was doing this to Reggie by having enough courage to go into the opposing locker room and point him out. And damn if he didn't drop 49 on us in Chicago later that month.

. . .

As I became established in the league, Michael and I didn't talk as much. We were from an era when your teammates were your best friends, and guys on another team were the enemy. We both thought like that.

When Michael temporarily left the NBA in 1993 to pursue a baseball career, the Houston Rockets teams of which I was a part began a run of back-to-back NBA championships. Michael returned in March 1995, and the Bulls lost to the Orlando Magic in the playoffs that year. We went on to beat Orlando in the Finals.

That summer, Michael was in Hollywood filming the movie *Space Jam*. He used his evenings to scrimmage with NBA players on a court that Warner Bros. had provided for them on their lot, in an effort to get back in shape. Reggie Miller, Patrick Ewing, Dennis Rodman—there was a lot of talent in those games.

The day I walked in to join, Michael was standing on the court.

"Tell everyone in Houston you all had your good time," he shouted.

"Oh no no," I said. "We won when you was here!"

He laughed and hugged me. And by the way, I was right. For decades, people have asked me if we would have won those titles had Michael not decided to temporarily retire. But what they often forget is that we did win after he came back.

That 1994–95 season, when he returned midway, the team wasn't as good as it had been or would be again. The big man Horace Grant had already gone to Orlando. Rodman, who would soon help launch another phase of the Bulls dynasty, was in San Antonio.

We never had the chance to play Jordan's Bulls head-to-head that year because they lost to the Magic in the playoffs. But I am convinced that if we had, we would have prevailed. We swept Orlando, after all.

Anyway, that day on the Warner Bros. lot was one of the few times Michael and I really connected during our many years in the league. We always enjoyed seeing each other at events back in North Carolina, but it wasn't like we were having vacations together, like players do now. Back then the NBA wasn't friendly like that.

Still, when I talked about Michael with family and friends I always spoke of a high level of respect, adulation, and love. But because we weren't that close or calling each other every day, I didn't know if he felt that way about me.

In 2009, Michael was about to be inducted into the Basketball Hall of Fame. I got a call from his assistant: "Michael wants to invite you to the Hall of Fame, because he feels you were instrumental in helping him get there."

"Really?" I said.

The assistant reiterated that Michael wanted me there, had the hotel all arranged for me, and was having a party afterward that he wanted me to attend.

Well, that's pretty cool that he would do that, I thought. *But maybe he is reaching out to all his teammates.*

When I got there, the entire group consisted of three or four guys from the Bulls, Sam Perkins, Buzz Peterson, and me. That was it.

TNT was covering the ceremony through its NBA TV network. They asked me to stop by and say something to their camera on my way in.

I walked down the red carpet and then found our reporter at a small table. After a minute or so of talking about what made Michael great, I heard a tremendous roar emerging from the crowd. Michael was walking up behind me. He stopped, grabbed my head, and kissed it.

"The best player in the world comes and kisses you on top of the head," I said. "It doesn't get any better than that."

It was flattering that he singled me out, but I thought that perhaps he was just euphoric in the moment as he walked into his Hall of Fame induction. Later, at the post-ceremony party, I pulled him aside.

"Hey, man, I just want to thank you for inviting me," I said. "We haven't played together or really talked—like, really *talked*—in a long time."

He was incredulous.

"What are you talking about?" he said. "Everything that you did in your freshman year and in your years at Carolina, I remember all that."

My face must have lit up with a massive smile.

"I never knew you talked about me the same way I talked about you, man," I said. "That makes me feel so much better."

He looked right at me.

"No, man," he said. "I love you."

This was a profound moment. A bond formed a generation earlier in North Carolina, when I recognized a special quality in Michael, was now coming full circle: he felt the connection to me, too.

CHAPTER TWO

JACK CURRAN

THE PUSH TO BE EXTRAORDINARY

It was not at all unusual for me to be sitting in Coach Jack Curran's office after school, as I was on this particular day. I did that all the time.

But as far as what he had to say to me—well, that was new, and it made me question everything about how I was preparing for my future.

I was a junior at Archbishop Molloy High School in Queens, fortunate enough to play for one of the top coaches in New York City history.

In his midfifties by then, Mr. Curran had been at the school since 1958, blazing a legendary trail. He won the city championship in basketball five times and in baseball seventeen times. He is the only coach to win the title in two sports during the same year—and he did that four times. He was inducted into nine different Halls of Fame.

He coached future NBA players Kenny Anderson, Kevin Joyce, Robert Werdann, Brian Winters, and me, and future New York Mets outfielder Mike Baxter. He would ultimately remain at the school for fifty-five years before passing away in 2013 at the age of eighty-two, winning more games across two sports than any coach in city history.

Even before I emerged as a top athlete, I became personally close to Mr. Curran. He was a mentor about all things basketball and life, and even enlisted me to answer his phone, which meant talking to the best college coaches in the country when they made their recruiting calls.

Sitting in his office this particular afternoon seemed no different than any other day. I had no idea that we were about to engage in a brief conversation that would change the trajectory of my life.

"Hey, Kenny," he said. "What are you planning on being?"

My answer came out quickly, like it does at a third-grade assembly when the teacher asks what you're going to do when you grow up.

"Coach, I wanna be in the NBA," I said.

His answer startled me.

"Oh, I didn't know that," Mr. Curran said. "You don't work hard enough to be an NBA player."

Wow.

Sometimes when teachers or coaches make statements like this, they're doing it as part of a strategy to motivate. That's not what this was. It was too matter-of-fact, and I knew Mr. Curran well enough that I could tell when he was saying something he truly believed.

It was as if I'd told him that I wanted to be an astronaut and he'd answered, "But you don't take any science classes."

Mr. Curran had coached both future NBA and Major League Baseball players. He knew what it took to get there, and it was obvious to him that I didn't have it, at least not yet.

.   .   .

It wasn't always smooth, shifting every day between the worlds of Archbishop Molloy and LeFrak City, Queens. When I first moved to LeFrak City, it was a predominantly upper-middle-class neighborhood, with a large number of white families still living there. Before long, though, there was an influx of Black families, who came because we were able to rent apartments at discounted rates.

My own family came from East New York, Brooklyn; let's just say that it wasn't the most affluent area. I sometimes hear others from the hood say that the environment ended up helping them, toughening them up and making them into the people they were. I never felt that way. In fact, I think it hindered me.

I made it in life, but I believe that if I'd had a different entry point into the world, that would have made it easier. I made it despite being in the hood, not because of it.

My mentality was always *I'm gonna go get it.*

And then it was *Damn, I've got to go around this to get it?*

"This" could refer to structural or institutional disadvantages inherent to someone with my background. Whatever you want to call it, it wasn't a straight path. But I went around the obstacles and got there anyway.

Even as LeFrak City itself became mostly populated with Black folks, the surrounding areas in Queens were extremely diverse from block to block. I could walk ten minutes and be in a predominantly Jewish neighborhood, then continue on to see any number of other racial and ethnic enclaves.

As a result, my childhood basketball teams reflected that diversity. Then at Archbishop Molloy, I was initially one of the few African Americans. The environment was not particularly diverse. This was an adjustment, but I loved to hoop. And sports was the great equalizer. The first time I hugged someone from another race was after hitting a game-winning shot. The only question within the ninety-four feet is, "Can you play?"

Still, race popped up as an issue from time to time, both in my awareness and in the behavior of other people. Freshman year, I didn't play varsity. I knew that to be great, playing varsity as a sophomore was going to be a must.

I had a very strong freshman season, and that summer I played with the Riverside Church AAU program, which at that time was famous for producing Division I players. I traveled all over the country to compete against some of the most elite high schoolers. I wasn't on the same level, but the experience gave me confidence that I could hold my own with the best.

Upon returning to school in the fall, I wanted to try out for varsity.

You know the saying that closed mouths don't get fed? Well, that's 100 percent true. My expectation was that Mr. Curran would ask me to play varsity. That was an unusual assumption, as most sophomores didn't play varsity at the time. But Coach had done it the previous year with a sophomore named Paul Baron, a forward who later attended Ohio University.

I just figured that Mr. Curran would hear about my improvement and ask me to move up.

That never happened. Weeks went by. Mr. Curran and I would talk, but never about me playing varsity.

Despite our burgeoning personal relationship, Mr. Curran was still larger than life to me. A New York City basketball legend, he had an aura about him that could be very intimidating. I was afraid to go into his office and ask him to play varsity. It was easier to ask a crush for a date.

Every day for two weeks, I would walk by his office after school, hoping that he would stop me and ask me to move up. One afternoon I went in, my heart pounding like a fist beating on a table.

"Mr. Curran," I said, "I'd like to try out for varsity this year."

His response was typical of him.

"Kenneth," he said, "if you think you're ready, then you should play varsity. See you next week."

It seemed like he'd been waiting on me the entire time. I walked out of his office, turned the corner, and started to yell and scream down the hallways of the school, pumping my fist as if I had just won an NCAA championship. But what I really won was the internal battle over pursuing what I wanted.

Once the season began, I was playing a lot. I would never start a game, because Mr. Curran had a rule that he wouldn't start anyone as an underclassman—but once I got in he never took me out. It was during these formative years that I earned the nickname "the Jet," because of my quickness.

The senior point guard was a white kid named Mark Carver, a good little player. He could shoot the ball and was quick, but I honestly felt that I was better than he was, even as a sophomore. Still, I was willing to wait my turn. In Coach Curran's book, only juniors and seniors could start—and I was going to go by his book.

One day when I was sitting in the office, Mark's older brother, who had played on the Archbishop Molloy team a few years earlier, walked in with Mr. Curran. Mark's brother asked if I could leave the office. I began to stand, but Mr. Curran objected.

"No, Kenneth can sit there," he said.

Reluctantly, Mark's older brother began to talk.

"I have a problem, Coach," he said. "Mark is a senior and Kenny is a sophomore. He has two years to get a scholarship. When Kenny comes into the game, he never comes out. I think Kenny should wait his turn to get more playing time, and Mark should get more."

I sat in the chair, quiet as could be. I was sixteen years old, and quite frankly a lot of things were rushing through my mind. I was the only Black kid playing major minutes on the varsity team, which was ranked in the city. I was at a Catholic private school and I wasn't Catholic. I was a sophomore and he was a senior.

It seemed that all the odds were stacked against me in this debate. Then Mr. Curran spoke.

"Carver," he said, "you won't have that problem anymore."

My heart sank. A small smile crossed Mark's brother's face. After a slight pause, Mr. Curran finished his thought.

"You won't have that problem because Mark is no longer on the team," he said.

I was floored. I had never seen that type of blunt honesty displayed from man to man—especially from white man to white man—to protect me, a Black kid.

"Coach, that's not what I'm saying," Mark's brother blurted before apologizing to Mr. Curran.

"No," Mr. Curran said. "You should apologize to Kenneth, because he actually deserves to start over Mark. Mark is lucky that I don't do that."

This was a lot to handle, because I actually did look up to Mark. He was a nice guy and never once gave me an inkling that he was jealous about my playing time.

Coach Curran showed me that day that he would stand up for me to the end. He also showed what an uncommonly no-nonsense person he was, refusing to bow to a family's demands. I have seen high school coaches get fired for that.

(An aside: Compare the story I just told you to an experience I had a few years back with my son KJ's team.

Andre Chevalier, who now coaches LeBron James's son Bronny at the high-profile Sierra Canyon private school in California, used to coach KJ at Oaks Christian School. At one point, Andre wasn't playing a senior point guard and nearly faced a mutiny for it.

During one of the games, the parents snuck away to a classroom and strategized about how to get Andre fired. They called me into the room. I thought we were going to talk about bringing snacks. When I saw what the meeting was actually about, I left immediately, saying that I couldn't be a part of anything like that.

"Andre," I texted the coach. "The craziest thing ever . . . they want you fired because you're not playing a kid! Come to room 310!!"

Granted, this was a totally different generation, one with helicopter parents, social media, and all kinds of variables that we couldn't have imagined when I was in high school. But I can't fathom Mr. Curran ever allowing that sort of thing to happen.)

The other time Mr. Curran sided with me against a fellow white man, it was an authority figure at the school. By the time I was a senior, I had become almost the face of Archbishop Molloy. As a first-team All-American, I was restoring the national spotlight to the school and its hallowed program. Stories in the media referred to me as "Kenny Smith, the guard from Archbishop Molloy."

I nevertheless had to study, of course, and deal with the same academic rigors as everyone else. In English, Brother John was a tough teacher, priding himself on the difficulty of the class. In turn, I took pride in making sure that I kept up good grades in addition to excelling on the basketball team.

But on one particular day, I forgot my homework sheet. That was a no-no in Brother John's class. Back in the eighties, corporal punishment was still allowed in parochial schools. For Brother John's class, if you forgot your homework, he would grab his wooden paddle off the desk and give you three smacks on the rear.

He was a little man, so it didn't really sting. The act was more about inflicting humiliation in front of your classmates. For maximum embarrassment, Brother John would do the paddling at the end of class, when other students were in the hallway and could stop at the window to look in.

"Mr. Smith," he said to me, "today you will be getting your first paddle in four years."

Then he began to laugh.

I did not think that I was above discipline because of my status as an athlete. But the punishment seemed unfair to me because of my academic performance. I had an A in the class and had never before missed an assignment. Brother John typically reserved this punishment for repeat offenders.

It seemed to me that he was eager to flex his power and show that regardless of the national attention I was receiving, he was still the boss. I saw the faces of my peers, their giggles and shock, and I decided: Brother John was not going to humiliate me.

But I also knew that if I started a confrontation, it would only make the situation worse. I whispered to my teammate Chris Sterling to go downstairs and let Coach Curran know that Brother John was going to give me the paddle after class.

"What the hell is Coach gonna do?" he whispered back.

"I don't know," I said. "But he should know about this."

Brother John was infamous around school for his paddle, and Mr. Curran was well aware of it. I suppose that I sensed he would recognize the unfairness of what was going on. He would never have abused his own power over a student like that.

Chris excused himself from class to use the restroom and ran down to Mr. Curran's office. As the period ended, there was still no sign of either of them.

The whole class began to murmur about what was about to happen. The student athlete of the year in New York, an academic All-American and first-team All-American in basketball, was about to get his butt paddled in front of the whole class and most of the school.

As I walked to the front of the class, the door opened. Mr. Curran walked in with Chris in tow. Brother John seemed surprised, but remained very cocky.

"Can I help you, Mr. Curran?" he said.

"No," Mr. Curran replied. "I'm going to help you. You will not paddle Kenneth in front of these students. He is the model student for Archbishop Molloy and brings a great deal of dignity, pride, and recognition to the school. He will not be humiliated in front of them. And if you have a problem with that, see me, and I have a paddle in my office as well for anyone who disagrees."

Everyone, including Brother John, was silent. Mr. Curran turned to me.

"Kenneth," he said, "let's go to practice."

I walked out of the room with him, never looking back at Brother John.

Mr. Curran had now taken his mentorship of me to another level—not only would he protect me, but he also acknowledged and showed respect for my accomplishments as a person. He had my back not just in front of Mark Carver's brother, but now in front of the entire faculty and my peers.

Remember, Archbishop Molloy at this time was more than 90 percent Caucasian. Mr. Curran showed time and again that this did not matter to him.

Not every adult at the school acted this way. At our graduation ceremony, I was sitting with my classmates while the principal handed out awards.

"And now we have our student athlete of the year," he said.

No one had told me about this award, but I was thinking that it had to be me. I had made the McDonald's All American Games and was headed to the University of North Carolina in the fall.

"Here's a young man who has brought a lot of attention to our school," he continued.

Now my heart stopped. *Damn,* I thought. *This is gonna be me.* I was getting excited.

"I just want to say," the principal concluded, "that this young man, when he was at our school for four years, made everyone not think of color—Kenny Smith."

I did not know how to take this. It was intended as a compliment, but it wasn't really a compliment at all. What would be wrong with people thinking of me as Black?

If you look at this from a 2023 lens, it's one of the most insulting things that he could have said. But you can't look at it from that lens, because it happened in 1983. In that context, a typical assumption about the Black kid was that he was from the ghetto, had no money, and acted a certain way. The principal saw it as a compliment to me that I didn't fit that stereotype.

The comment has stuck with me for all these years. When people talk about the African American community, what really gets under our skin is when other groups see us from a limited point of view.

We're a very complex people. What you might see reflected on TV or in movies is just one point of view. So when the principal of the school essentially said that I didn't fit his definition of Black, it was a way to simplify me. But I came from the melting pot of New York and wasn't a product of Black culture alone.

In Queens I was surrounded by Jewish and Chinese neighborhoods. I could smell the spices of Indian food and I could go get a Jamaican patty. If I just wanted to stay within my four blocks and be Kenny Smith—hip-hop, Run-DMC, LL Cool J—I could do that all day. But that wasn't me.

I would venture out of the four blocks and hear Led Zeppelin and Pink Floyd. One of the dudes on my team was big into Floyd's album *The Wall*.

"Yo, what's that?" I said one day when he played it. "That beat's got a bounce to it. It sounds great."

A fashion statement for the rock guys at Archbishop Molloy was to take a denim jacket and have an album cover painted onto the back. One of the guys gave me his Pink Floyd *The Wall* jacket because I kept telling him how dope it looked. I wore it proudly with my Kangol hat, gold rope chain, and name belt buckle because I loved all of it.

You could see a similar type of cultural mash-up in the stands at our games. Our gym held about 600 people, and there would be 850 trying to get in. Our mascot was a lion who beat on a drum. There was no band, just that *boom boom boom* of the drum and the packed, frenzied crowd.

It was mostly white, reflecting the makeup of the school. But then there was an interesting mix with the LeFrak City folks.

One of my dad's good friends was Pierre Turner, a prominent judge who lived near us. He'd be sitting alongside guys who I knew sold drugs, and others who were from Mafia families. And everyone was high-fiving. The game was attracting everyone in my neighborhood.

Every few games I would look up to see the same kids who would drive by and call you the N-word on the street hugging Black kids when we'd score. I would just laugh. Everyone who is good ain't all good, and everyone who is bad ain't all bad, you know? When it came to people like that, I saw a difference between being racist and being racial.

A racist is someone with the power to hinder what I'm doing, like preventing me from living in their building or getting a certain job. Racial, to me, involves making comments. It's a bad habit, often learned from parents. Racial comments can make you feel very angry, but I could tell who was a true racist and who wasn't at that level.

And the beautiful thing about spending every day from nine a.m. to three p.m. at Archbishop Molloy and three p.m. to nine a.m. in LeFrak City was that it gave me an ability to understand anyone—even those who made racial comments—because there was nothing new under the sun. Whatever a person was like, I'd already met someone similar.

Anyway, I got a kick out of meeting these tough guys from different ethnic groups. We had some real characters at the school.

We had one kid who was from a known Mafia family. One day he got into an argument with another guy in the rec room, and a scuffle broke out. It wasn't that big a fight, and the teachers broke it up, but the kid got hit in just the right place to end up with a swollen eye.

The next morning, I was walking to school from the train station and saw five black limousines lined up in front of the building. I figured that the mayor was visiting.

The windows of the cars were tinted black. When one of them rolled down, I saw the kid with the swollen eye. Let's call him Johnny. We were on friendly terms—he was a nice kid who just happened to be from a particular background—so I said hello.

"Hey, wassup, Johnny!"

Normally he would return the greeting, but this time he said nothing. Then every other window in his limo rolled down. Johnny pointed past me and said, "That's him."

I looked to see the kid who had given him the swollen eye. Three car doors opened, and a big guy got out of each of them.

"Hey, come here," one of the guys said. "Do you know who this is?"

The poor kid was like, "I'm sorry! I'm sorry! I didn't know!"

"If you ever touch him again," the guy said, "you'll be in the East River with some cement shoes."

It sounded like a line from a movie, but he really did say it. And with a strong New York accent—like *sea*-ment.

Holy shit! I thought.

I never forgot that phrase. I still say it to Charles Barkley when he gets on my bad side: "You're gonna be in the river with *sea*-ment shoes, Chuck!" Ha-ha-ha.

This was a great example of how growing up in Queens helped me to relate to other groups. I'd see Italian kids on the train with their jewelry out, proud and confident just like us.

They didn't have any fear, the same way we didn't. You know that Public Enemy song "Fear of a Black Planet"? Well, they didn't have any fear of a Black planet and we didn't have any fear of an Italian planet. It was more like, "Nah, we're good, and you're good, too." There was actually a deep sense of connection when you looked past the surface.

. . .

Back to the time that Mr. Curran told me I didn't work hard enough to play in the NBA. He was a no-nonsense person, honest but never brutal. His was a gentle honesty.

The difference between brutal honesty and gentle honesty is that the former is intended to hold a person back. Gentle honesty has the intention to propel. When he made that comment, I was just a blip on the radar—a good player, but not the best in the city.

My junior year, I'd undergone the previously mentioned arthroscopic knee surgery and had a lackluster season, averaging 16 points per game. Coach would say that there was a 16-point scorer on every team in America, because someone had to score.

I had some interest from colleges, but no concrete offers. Mr. Curran was right: I wasn't NBA material yet, or even a top college prospect. I was talented and likable enough to become a big fish in a small pond, and this had kept me from pushing myself.

Now I understood that I had to work harder. I vowed that a conversation like that would never happen again. In figuring out how to deal with that uneasy feeling, I began to really look at and think about the word "extraordinary."

It dawned on me that to take my game to the next level, I just needed to do the ordinary things a bit extra. Don't rest on my laurels or rely on natural ability. It was that simple.

I started taking extra jump shots and layups, running extra laps, jumping rope a few extra times. Instead of taking the elevator up to our twelfth-floor apartment, I walked up the extra stairs. And I studied a little extra, too. All in an effort to become extraordinary.

My brother Vince, who is like a basketball Rain Man, helped me with the process. He came up with ball-handling drills and workout ideas that helped me rehab my knee and improve my game at the same time.

Mr. Curran had given me the push I needed at the perfect moment. My appreciation for that lasted a lifetime and resulted in me naming my son Malloy after the school. That was really a tribute to Mr. Curran himself. The name "Jack" didn't seem quite right for us, so we landed on a slightly modified spelling of the school, with Coach in mind.

He and I remained in close touch for the rest of his life, talking once or twice a week. When he died, his niece gave me one of his ties. This was a great honor, because he only had like four ties.

The summer after my junior year, I went from being a blip on the radar to the top guard in New York City, along with Pearl Washington from Boys and Girls High School, who later starred at Syracuse.

I became a McDonald's All American, one of the top ten players in the country. In 2012, I was voted one of the top thirty-five McDonald's All Americans of all time. This leap happened after Mr. Curran gave me that brief but impactful talk. In less than six months, I had changed the perception of who I was just by doing things a little bit extra.

Dean Smith, my legendary coach from the University of North Carolina, used to call Mr. Curran every year.

"Are there any players in the New York City area that could play at the University of North Carolina?" he would ask.

During my freshman, sophomore, and junior years, Mr. Curran had told him no. When Coach Smith called the next time with the question, he heard a different answer.

"Yes," said Mr. Curran. "I have a rising senior at Archbishop Molloy who will interest you."

Surprised, Coach Smith asked if this player had transferred in.

"No," said Mr. Curran. "He's been here the whole time, but I've never seen a kid improve from one year to the next as much as this one has. His name is Kenneth Smith. He'll be your starting point guard next year if you recruit him."

The rest, as they say, is history.

CHAPTER THREE

DEAN SMITH

WHITE PRIVILEGE

The year 2021 started off with a bang, and not in a good way.

On Thursday, January 6, as Congress was about to affirm Joe Biden's victory in the presidential election, a violent mob loyal to President Donald Trump stormed the U.S. Capitol. It was a stunning attempt to overturn America's democratic process.

These armed terrorists clearly believed that the revolution had come. As we watched the unsettling events unfold, I had the same thought that many Black Americans did: I was not surprised.

We also asked ourselves why a crowd of predominantly white people was met with such a different level of force, or lack thereof, than Black Americans typically are. Although, truth be told, we weren't surprised by that either.

Among the many other revealing aspects of the insurrection was the clear view it provided of white privilege.

These pro-Trump riots showed quite a contrast to the previous July, when a group of Black Lives Matter demonstrators in the same city were met with guns, rubber bullets, and tear gas. That was white privilege working overtime for them.

Taking this all in, my mind drifted that day to thoughts of Dean Smith, the iconic coach at the University of North Carolina. The concept of white privilege has been in our collective consciousness a lot over the past few years, but Coach Smith was decades ahead of his time in intuitively understanding how to use his own privilege for good.

He had an instinct for justice, took action in pursuit of that goal, and encouraged us to do the same. With the nation in crisis, this was who I wanted to talk to.

If I had been able to consult with Coach—who passed away in 2015—he would have said, "What are you going to do during these times, this insurrection, this inequality? How are you going to make a change in your house, and how are you going to make a change nationally? You have a national platform. Are you going to do something with it?"

Coach Smith's résumé is well known to any basketball fan. Two national championships and eleven appearances in the Final Four. A pioneer of civil rights in the college game. As legendary a coach as has ever lived.

To me, he was much more than that. He was a communicator and teacher at the level of other great historical figures. I'm talking about Gandhi, Mother Teresa, Martin Luther King Jr. That's not hyperbole. That's who Coach Smith was to me. I think about him often, but he was especially on my mind during the riot at the Capitol.

There was a time back in the day at UNC when we passed by anti-apartheid protesters on campus.

"What are you going to do, Kenny?" Coach asked in his low-key but probing way.

"What do you mean?" I said.

"As a young African American man who is on this campus, what are you going to do?"

And that was it. He would follow it up with a casual, "OK, I'll talk to you later," and leave you thinking.

If Coach had been around in 2020, when I walked off the TNT set in solidarity with BLM protesters, he would have been proud and excited.

Martin Luther King Jr. said, "If you want to say that I was a drum major, say that I was a drum major for justice. Say that I was a drum major for peace. I was a drum major for righteousness. And all of the other shallow things will not matter."

Coach Smith was a drum major for justice. And one of the most profound influences on my life.

.   .   .

Our family originates from St. George, South Carolina, the place that is also the origin of my understanding of how deep racism runs in our country.

Even though I'm a proud native New Yorker, I spent a lot of summers in that small southern town, population 2,500, with my father's mom, Grandma Agnes.

My grandma was born in the year 1900. Her parents lived in the era of slavery, which was abolished in the United States in 1865.

Think about that. I, Kenny "the Jet" Smith, high school All-American, college basketball player of the year, two-time NBA champion, part of the Emmy-winning show *Inside the NBA,* am only one generation removed from direct experience with slavery.

I mean that literally: my father's grandfather was a slave. Crazy, right? When you have that so recently in your family tree—when my children can sit around the dinner table with someone whose grandparent was born into slavery—racism is not an abstract concept. We can feel the violence and oppression in our bones.

Because of that, our dinner conversations were much different than any that my white friends were having. Even those who understood racism could not have had slavery in their blood like we did.

This foundational difference helped me to understand what to expect from America, and specifically from white Americans. Still, when I looked around New York, I saw that many races could be successful or affluent.

My mom would always say, "Kenny, you can be whatever you want to be," and that seemed validated by what I noticed around me. Many of our dinner conversations would start with me talking about my aspirations of being president one day. (Yes, Barack beat me to it.)

But when I went to spend those summers in St. George, a different reality revealed itself, one that highlighted poverty, fear, and racism. Blacks and whites lived in separate parts of town. My aunts and uncles had zero white friends. My cousins had zero white friends. My friends had zero white friends.

This was the 1970s. Civil rights, back of the bus—that stuff hadn't changed down south. The only thing that had changed was that the sign telling you not to drink out of the water fountain wasn't there. But it wasn't like you were going to drink out of that water fountain anyway. You just knew.

You didn't go into certain stores. You had to wait outside. I would walk in with my friends and they would say, "We've got to wait until these people leave," then turn right back around and stand outside until the other Black people were done in the store.

Did they have a sign that read, "Only a certain number of Blacks in my store"? No. But only two or three Black people were allowed in that store at one time.

The old rules were still in place because many of the people who were in charge before the civil rights movement still retained their power. It felt more than passive-aggressive. It was aggressive. And it was so frustrating.

Mentally and emotionally, this did two things. At first it made me feel put down, like I was worth less than white people. Then, at fourteen or fifteen years old, I started to feel power in the fact that they were nervous around me.

Oh, they're scared of me, I would think. *They're afraid to have more than three of me in the store.*

This is who I was when I met Coach Smith during the recruiting process: increasingly aware of racism, especially in the South, and working through my own reactions to it.

When Coach came for his home visit, he couldn't have looked more out of context: walking into LeFrak City, my brick high-rise apartment complex in Queens, he seemed like pure country.

He had perfectly coiffed gray hair. He wore argyle golf pants that must have had seven different colors stitched together. The whole package made me think of Colonel Sanders, and here I was in New York City styling myself after LL Cool J. How was this going to fit?

That southern stereotype lasted only until he started talking. Coach was understated and caring, and not a salesman. He covered every topic but basketball—academics, the campus, you name it.

Finally, my dad said, "Hey, uh, Coach Smith. A lot of the coaches come here and project how much my son will play his freshman year. Some say he will start, some say he'll be a reserve."

"Mr. Smith," Coach said, "I never promise playing time. But I do promise that if your son is one of the five best players, he'll be on the court."

That struck me. No one had said that.

Coach went on: "But I will guarantee your son has a great experience at our university."

And that was the end of the basketball talk. He returned to telling me about academics.

The other coach with whom I'd had a strong relationship during the recruiting process was Lou Carnesecca at St. John's, but he was a city guy. I knew a million fast-talking Lou Carneseccas.

"Hey, what's up, Kenny, you're gonna come here and eat pasta?" he'd say.

With Coach Smith it wasn't, "You're gonna come here and eat southern fried chicken?"

He would just talk to you. And to me that was the most comforting feeling. Somebody was just looking at me as me. There was no salesmanship.

His underlying premise was like, *I'm a Bentley. If you can't see that I'm a Bentley and you don't want to drive in this, I'm not going to convince you. You don't need rims, you don't need anything. It's a Bentley. If you can't see that it's a Bentley, then something is wrong with you.*

To this day, that approach influences my own. I'm not a seller of myself. If you can't see what I offer? All right. It's OK. Because I'm not selling it.

What Dean Smith had to offer was not for sale either. While this immediately impressed me, I still didn't know much about Coach or his impact. Growing up in New York, I was an NBA fan and had minimal awareness of college basketball. This was Walt "Clyde" Frazier's town.

The one exception to that was Georgetown University and its legendary coach John Thompson. He was the epitome of what every African American kid wanted to be around. He was fierce. He was unapologetic. He was regal in being Black.

If you followed rap music and were an inner-city kid, you were like, "Georgetown, John Thompson, that's my guy." That would be a recruiting tool for him.

Coach Smith could have answered that with his own sales pitch to Black athletes, if he had chosen to.

In 1967, Coach recruited Charlie Scott, a guard out of New York

City, and made him the first Black scholarship athlete in North Carolina history. At no point during his home visit or on my subsequent trip to campus had he mentioned that.

If he had, I would have said, *Wait, you're the first coach to bring a Black player to North Carolina and the ACC? What? Oh, you're one of us!*

This was an important concept. As an African American player getting to know a white authority figure, you're always wondering, *Is this guy one of us?*

Coach Smith could have name-dropped Charlie Scott and cleared that up right away. From my experience in South Carolina as a kid, I could imagine the pushback he had to endure when he advocated for Charlie. We know what it looks like when somebody is standing next to us who doesn't look like us. We appreciate that pressure.

But Coach never mentioned this history the whole time I was there. As he was driving me back to the airport, chatting about how it went, I just had to ask him.

"Coach," I said, "why didn't you ever bring up Charlie Scott?"

Coach shrugged off my question, but I pressed.

"Seriously, that's kind of a big deal what you did, isn't it?" I said.

"I didn't recruit a Black athlete," he finally said. "I recruited Charlie."

Whoa, I thought. *I'm definitely coming here.*

. . .

My relationship with Coach only deepened once I arrived on campus and started to settle in.

Practices at North Carolina were a marvel to behold. Coach planned every moment, posted a detailed schedule, and expected us to conduct each drill with precision. But it wasn't just a basketball exercise. We also had a "thought of the day," a quote or statement that Coach felt was meaningful.

Each player not only had to memorize the thought of the day but recite it when called upon. This could be in the middle of sprints, drills, anything.

It would be funny to see some of the greatest young players in the world panting and sweating while screaming out poetry or quotes from great leaders: *Never judge a man unless you've walked in his moccasins for at least two moons! The foundation of love is stronger than the building of hate!*

At times we would have visitors at practice, friends and family along with the NBA scouts who flocked into the corridors of the gym. Once, when my brother Vince attended, I told him to close his eyes for one minute.

After practice I asked, "When you closed your eyes, could you tell who the best players were by the sound of Coach Smith's voice?"

Vince said that he could not tell if Coach was talking to Michael Jordan, Sam Perkins, or the last man on the team. This taught me that leadership allows each team member to feel valued, no matter their role.

Coach created a chemistry that allowed the group to self-monitor, self-police, and respect one another the way he respected all of us. And this didn't only win him favor with the lesser players. The stars also responded to the lack of preferential treatment.

Jordan once said to me, "Smith, you know I don't make one important decision in my life without running it by Coach?"

Mike was thirty-two at the time. I looked at him and said, "Neither do I."

As the point guard, I did receive priceless individual attention in the form of pregame strategy meetings with Coach. One of the first came toward the end of training camp during my freshman year. It was not my proudest moment, but of course I walked away from it having learned something.

In training camp, we had a blue team and a white team. The white team consisted of the starters, while the blue team was for guys expected to come off the bench. A few weeks into camp, I felt like I was killing it but would never be on the white team. After a while it made me wonder where I stood.

Then, in an intrasquad scrimmage in front of the whole school, I scored 25 points. Not even that was enough to get me off the blue team.

Now I was like, *What is going on here? Coach told me the five best players were going to start.*

By the fourth week of camp, we were getting close to the first game and I still hadn't been on the white team. *Man,* I thought. *I don't even know what I'm busting my butt for.*

I started to give less than 100 percent in practice. Coach called me into his office.

"Kenny, are you OK?" he said.

"Yeah, I'm OK."

"Are you homesick, or did something happen at school . . ."

I was cocky enough at that age to just come out with it.

"Honestly, Coach," I said. "I'm killing these guys at practice and I haven't been on the white team yet. I don't understand."

"Oh," he said. "So that's why you were kind of going through the motions?"

"Yeah!"

"Kenny," he said, "I brought you in here because I was going to tell you that you were going to start—as a freshman—in the first exhibition game and then in the first game of the season. But you know what? Now, if you work hard this week, we'll see what happens."

Noooo, I thought. *Why didn't you keep your mouth shut? Why didn't you just keep working hard?*

Coach had noticed my hard work. I should have just kept at it and remained focused. Instead, I sulked.

Because of that, I didn't start in the exhibition game. But I did start the opener and from then was on the white team permanently, and I didn't look back.

For about twenty minutes before every game we would sit in his office. It started as basketball talk: "OK, what plays are we running today? What do you think? What do you see? Why do you think I'm doing what I'm doing?"

But as the year went on, we began to drift into conversations about life off the court.

"Oh," he might say, perusing the list of players' ticket requests. "Now, Kenny, I see you've got a new girl you're dating. She's on this list every day. Who's Dawn? Is it serious?"

"Yeah, well," I'd say, all sheepish, "me and Dawn are dating."

By senior year, those conversations came to encompass every topic you could imagine. He knew more about me than my roommate did.

That was highly unusual among top college coaches of that era, or probably any era. I know a lot of great players who came out of prestigious programs, and to a man they always say that what they envy most about Carolina is the relationship we had with Coach Smith.

As one friend told me, "Honestly, I could call my coach and say, 'My dog died, my wife left me, and I got shot in the foot,' and he'd say, 'Man, did you see our game last night?' "

Once Coach Smith got to know me, he was also better able to steer me. His techniques were subtle but masterful.

When I was a senior, I was selected to the Playboy All-American team. Not only was it an honor to be named the top guard in the country, but the process included a photo shoot at the Playboy Mansion. Now, I was a young man, and a visit to Hugh Hefner's house did not sound like a bad idea at all.

At the time, Coach's wife, the psychiatrist Dr. Linnea Smith, was outspoken about *Playboy*'s involvement in the All-American selection process. She objected to what she saw as the magazine's promotion of sexuality and drug use.

Despite this, Coach did not tell me to decline. He was a devout Christian, but true to character, he wasn't one to sell his religion to you, or force it on you.

Instead, he would offer it to you. Unlike some coaches, he didn't have a rule that players had to attend church on Sundays. He merely required that you had a note from your parents excusing you. Now, what parent is going to write their kid that note? Pretty clever strategy by Coach.

After being selected as a Playboy All-American, I sat in his office.

"Kenny," he said, "do you really want to go to the Playboy Mansion with Hugh Hefner?"

My mind was screaming *YES!* but my answer was more restrained.

"Coach, I made first team," I said. "I want to go. I want to take the pictures and be in the magazines and tell people I made Playboy All-American."

He knew what I was really excited about, but he played it cool.

"Well," he said, "I'm not going to say you shouldn't go."

"Coach, if you were first-team All-American, would you go?" I asked.

"Personally? No, I wouldn't go, because of my beliefs," he said.

This was a smooth move. All of a sudden, I could hear my mom scolding: *Kenny, what are you doing at the Playboy Mansion?*

Dang, I thought. *I shouldn't have asked him that question.*

"How about this," he said. "I see you want to go, but let's act as if you're not going for a moment. Let's tell them you're not going to go, and see what they say. Because if you're first-team All-American, you should still be recognized as one of the best players in the country, regardless of whether you're at the Playboy Mansion or not. So let's make the call."

I agreed, and he called up the folks at *Playboy*.

"Kenny won't be able to be at the photo shoot due to his beliefs," he told them.

"If he can't come, he can't be first-team All-American," they said. "He can't be in the back of the magazine."

Coach put the call on hold and said to me, "What you accomplished shouldn't be diminished if you can't be at that shoot."

Playboy's answer bothered me, too. I thought, *Wait a minute. I killed the whole ACC this year, the whole country. But I'm not first-team now if I won't go to the Playboy Mansion?*

"Oh, I get it," I said.

Coach saw through the whole thing. *Playboy* didn't care about me. They just wanted to use me. I didn't go to the shoot—and it was my decision, not his.

.   .   .

The lessons we learned from Coach were not, of course, confined to off-the-court issues. He taught us about ourselves during competition, too.

During my freshman year, we were playing Duke University. We were the number one team in the country, undefeated in ACC play, but the Blue Devils were on the rise.

Mike Krzyzewski—"Coach K"—was building the foundation of what we now know as one of the great programs. He already had standout players like Johnny Dawkins, Jay Bilas, and Tommy Amaker.

But while Duke was on the rise, we were still the gold standard of college basketball, the team by which everyone measured themselves. We had ten high school All-Americans who played hard, smart, and together.

The game was close through the first half, but the second half started in a blizzard for us. I threw the ball inside to Sam Perkins, our four-time All-American, and he missed an easy layup.

Duke returned with a tough fall-away shot by Dawkins. I missed a wide-open jumper, then Bilas hit a shot while falling out of bounds.

Michael Jordan missed his patented turnaround jumper, and Dawkins converted an errant pass from Amaker into an unbelievable reverse layup. I looked over at the scoreboard: we were down 15 points with ten minutes to go.

The Duke fans, affectionately known as the Cameron Crazies, were living up to their name by going nuts. I looked at Coach and asked if he wanted a time out.

His mood did not seem to match the moment. He sat with his legs crossed, looking relaxed and shaking his head no. I was perplexed. No time out? Down 15, crowd going wild?

This was one of my first nationally televised games. My friends and family were watching, and I didn't want to be embarrassed.

"Ten-minute drill!" Coach yelled.

He had offensive and defensive schemes for ten minutes, eight minutes, six minutes, and two minutes. As a point guard, I had specific data on which plays to run during those times. We drilled them every day at the end of practice. This time, we ran the ten-minute drill and came back to win the game in regulation.

On the bus ride back to Chapel Hill, I asked Coach why he hadn't wanted a time out to settle us down.

"What was I going to tell you all?" he said. "Stop missing great shots? I knew things would level off if we continued to play the right way. And if not, I was prepared to shake their hands and walk off. I also knew we had prepared for these moments in our ten-minute drill segments."

Our assistant coach Roy Williams—later the longtime head coach and a legend in his own right—overheard the conversation.

"Son," he said to me, "I was thinking the same thing. Then Coach leaned over to us and said, 'Now is when our preparation kicks in.'"

Coach always talked about competition like that. It was never "winning" or "losing." He didn't say, "Let's win today."

He said, "Let's play our game." He was comfortable with any outcome, as long as we could hold our heads high.

．　　．　　．

When many of my white friends ask me about the Black Lives Matter movement, they typically pose a question: What can they do?

My view on this is slightly contrarian. It's not my obligation to tell them what is needed. As a Black American, I feel that we are the truest Americans. We've fought in wars and we've protested peacefully. We have struggled to have our points heard and given our lives to a country that hasn't always given great things back to us.

I don't think it's the job of the oppressed to bear the burden of also describing our needs. Coach Smith grasped the key point that it wasn't on the Black athlete to explain it to him. It was his job to learn.

One of my favorite Tar Heels, Makhtar N'Diaye, came to UNC much later than I did. Makhtar is originally from Senegal, and the only transfer student that Coach Smith ever took from another Division I program. At first, he was still trying to get used to the culture, and the coaches were working to understand where he was coming from.

One day Makhtar was having a tough practice, which isn't unusual for any player at North Carolina. Practicing against the likes of Vince Carter and Antawn Jamison daily is not easy.

Bill Guthridge, an assistant coach, stopped practice and asked Makhtar if he thought his effort had been good enough. At North Carolina we knew that was a rhetorical question. You just shake your head no and try to do better.

But Makhtar's response was different. He did not look at Coach Guthridge or acknowledge the question. This infuriated the coach.

"Makhtar, pay attention," he barked.

No response. So Coach Guthridge threw him out of practice. Afterward, Coach Smith summoned Makhtar to his office.

"Is everything OK?" he asked. "Are you homesick? Having personal issues?"

Through all of this, Makhtar refused to look at Coach.

"Makhtar, look at me when I'm talking to you," Coach said. He wasn't a yeller and never cursed, but this was loud and firm by his standards.

Finally, Makhtar looked up and said, "Coach, in my culture it's a sign of disrespect to look an adult in the eye."

"Oh, OK," Coach said, calm again. "Have a great day, Makhtar."

Flash forward to the off-season, when Coach Guthridge vanished from campus for a few days. Makhtar didn't think much of it, but at one point he called his parents in Senegal to check in. His mom answered.

"Hey, Makhtar," she said. "A man is here who says he's your assistant coach at the university. Did you do something wrong? He's here eating with us and talking to us."

Coach Smith had sent Coach Guthridge to Senegal.

"I wanted him to learn your culture, so we would never make that mistake again," he later told Makhtar.

When Coach Guthridge returned from his trip, that five-foot-nine white man from Parsons, Kansas, was wearing a dashiki. He hugged Makhtar. That's the essence of change: understanding.

I'm a big fan of the musician Gil Scott-Heron. He coined the phrase "The revolution will not be televised," meaning that social justice would not be something you'd see on TV. It would be a shift that people felt internally. They would realize that they were on the wrong side and make a change. It happened in small human moments.

Coach Smith understood all this intuitively. He understood the revolution.

. . .

On October 7, 1997, my phone rang. It was Coach.

"Hey, Kenny," he said. "I just want to tell you that I'm going to hold a press conference today to announce that I'm retiring."

"I appreciate the call, Coach," I said. "You didn't have to do that."

"And," he said, "I also wanted to apologize."

"Apologize?" I said. "For what?"

I couldn't fathom what this great man could possibly have to be sorry about.

"Well, Kenny," he said, "I wanted Phil Ford to take over for me, and Coach Guthridge was going to retire. But they wouldn't give the job to Phil because he had a DUI. I want to apologize to you because, for everything the Black athlete has done for this university, the next coach should have been African American."

This amazed me. Who thought like that, on a day that was supposed to be a celebration of his own career?

"Well, Coach, I appreciate you saying that, but I understand," I said. "Phil has had some transgressions. It's OK."

But he was insistent. "No," he said, "I'm just really upset that they wouldn't hire him."

That was Coach in a nutshell: understanding something that was bigger than he was. It wasn't even me who didn't get the job; it was Phil Ford. To apologize to me as a Black athlete—that's next-level thought.

When Coach passed away in 2015, some of his former players received a letter expressing gratitude for what we had done for the university and for him personally. The envelope also contained a check for three hundred dollars, along with simple instructions: he wanted us to have dinner on him.

He was literally dying—and thinking of us instead of himself. Now every year during the Final Four, I host a dinner for every player from North Carolina who is in town for the event.

In so many ways, I'm trying to pay it forward for Coach Smith. I just hope I can live up to his example.

CHAPTER FOUR

BILL RUSSELL

GOOD TROUBLE

At twelve thirty a.m. one night during my rookie season with the Kings, I was in the passenger seat of a car driving down Interstate 5 in Sacramento.

Then came the bright lights that no Black male wants to see. A police car was pulling us over.

Nervous, I looked at the driver, who was also a Black man. But he was cool as a cucumber. Actually, he continued driving.

"Aren't you going to pull over?" I said.

"Yeah," he said. "When I get closer to home."

Then he laughed. My heart dropped. What was I getting myself into, riding with this guy?

As a twenty-one-year-old New Yorker, I was very accustomed to being stopped or seeing my friends detained because they—ahem—looked the part. The stop-and-frisk program had not been officially implemented then, but "driving while Black" has been risky in New York City for a long time.

The New York City Police Department's practice of temporarily detaining, questioning, and at times searching civilians and suspects on the street for weapons and other contraband was known in other places in the United States as the Terry stop. Officers could do this based on the mere suspicion that a person was committing a crime.

Many years later, this practice was finally ended because of the racial profiling it promoted. (Just for the record, statistics make clear that African Americans do not use or sell drugs or commit crimes at a higher rate than white Americans.)

We don't have to memorize facts like the incarceration rate of Black males to understand that, systematically, we're getting the short end of the stick.

Growing up, I walked through some of the toughest neighborhoods in Brooklyn, the Bronx, and Harlem to basketball games at all hours of the day and night. I've never been robbed or mugged, nor have I ever broken the law other than a traffic ticket.

But I have twice had guns drawn on me and felt afraid for my life. Both times, the aggressors were not robbers or drug dealers but police officers. Both instances began as routine stop and frisks— those "you look like you're up to something" conversations that we all know too well.

My strategy for navigating around this harassment was to always carry my basketball. Apparently, if I took it out and started dribbling, I didn't look like I was up to something anymore. I took to carrying it even when I wasn't going to a game or practice. The ball became my gun. It protected me against harassment and embarrassment.

When an officer did hassle me, the interaction usually ended with him going through my bag, finding the ball, and letting me go.

Those experiences were my context for that night in Sacramento, and the reason why I was so nervous as we continued to roll along in a BMW with no basketball in the back seat. I knew what could happen.

The driver continued for another minute, then finally pulled over. Now my adrenaline was pumping. I knew the routine: keep your hands on the steering wheel and dashboard and don't move. The driver obviously didn't know the rules. Still calm and confident, he started to reach for his license.

The white officer approached the car. Had the officer been Black, I still would have felt the fear. But a white cop—well, I knew the drill by now.

The driver rolled down his window.

"Do you know how fast you were going?" the officer said. "Are you in a rush? Don't you realize if you're driving that fast—"

Before the officer could get out another word, the driver interrupted.

"Listen," he said. "Either you're gonna give me a lecture or a ticket, but you're not giving me both."

I was floored. I had never heard anyone speak to an officer as if the officer was a man with limited power.

"License and registration," the cop said.

Then: "Oh, sorry, Mr. Russell. Great game tonight, guys. Slow down and have a nice night."

Bill Russell, the NBA icon and head coach of my team, looked at me and launched into his famous high-pitched cackle. But as we drove away, his laughter stopped and his tone turned serious.

"You've done nothing wrong, Kenny," he said. "Never let them think you have. And always make them respect you."

. . .

You're probably wondering why, as a twenty-one-year-old rookie, I was riding home with Coach.

(I still call him Coach to this day, by the way—a designation that I only give to certain coaches. "Coach" means mentor, life teacher, and basketball expert. Charles Barkley knows my rule and always notices whom I call "Coach" and which so-called coaches I refer to by name. He gets a real kick out of that.)

Bill Russell was as towering a legend as the NBA had, both on and off the court. One of the top rebounders of all time, he was captain of an Olympic gold medal–winning team, a five-time Most Valuable Player, twelve-time All-Star, and eleven-time NBA champion.

He was the league's first Black superstar, and when Celtics coach Red Auerbach retired in 1966, Russell became the first Black coach in modern American professional sports. He found immediate success in that role, winning two titles as a player-coach.

In retirement, he enjoyed a broadcasting career and a successful run as coach and general manager of the Seattle SuperSonics, whom he guided to consecutive playoff appearances in 1975 and 1976. The Kings hired him in 1987.

Playing during the civil rights era in Boston, a city with a history of racial division, Coach Russell had a complicated relationship with Celtics fans. Outspoken about racism from a young age, he endured constant taunts and slurs. In 1963, his house was broken into and racist graffiti was written on the walls. The intruder even defecated on his bed.

Those experiences had hardened Coach Russell and surely contributed to his gruff demeanor. But while Coach's style wasn't for everyone, my time with him was transformative. He taught me to be a professional and showed me what it looked like to be a strong, self-assured Black man.

Coach chose me sixth overall in the 1987 NBA draft and took a keen interest in me from the very beginning. At the start of our first road trip, he stopped me when I was getting on the team bus.

"Hey, Kenny, sit next to me," he said.

At that age, the last place I wanted to sit was next to the coach. I was more inclined to head straight to the back of the bus, telling jokes and playing cards with the guys.

Then he added, "Also, I believe we live near each other, so you'll be riding home with me at the end of every trip."

"Coach," I said, "if it's OK, I'd rather sit in the back with the players."

He stood in the aisle, looked toward the back, and put his arm around my shoulder.

"Excuse me," he said, loud enough for everyone to hear. "I'm letting Kenny here understand something."

He pointed toward one particular player.

"You see him?" Coach said. "He's a loser."

Then he started gesturing to other guys.

"The guy back there? He's a loser. That guy? He's a loser, too. If you want to be a champion, Kenny—if you want to be a winner—you sit next to me. You make the choice."

I stood there, stunned by how he had disrespected those players. The choice was clear. Now sheepish, I plopped down in the seat next to him.

"OK," Coach yelled to the back of the bus. "Carry on!"

He turned to me. "What would you have done if I called you out like that?" he said.

"I would have been very upset," I said. "I would have told you that I'm no loser, and that you must be talking to the wrong guy."

"Exactly," he said. "That's why you're sitting next to me. Those guys didn't say anything. Now I know they really are losers."

He punctuated that statement with his high-pitched cackle.

So there I was, relegated to sitting next to the teacher for the rest of the season. These were the days before teams chartered private jets. We traveled commercial, usually on early morning flights, out to the next city. Sometimes I would nod off, and Coach would nudge me awake.

"Sleep nights, young fella," he'd say. "Listen to what I'm saying."

I became Coach's shadow, hearing all the great stories about the Celtics and civil rights. Coach Russell had a dual role with the organization, also running the front office. He would often spend flights reviewing paperwork about upcoming games, scouting reports, and other team business.

On one flight I happened to glance over.

"Man, Coach, that's a lot of work," I said. "What are you doing?"

"I'm looking at players from overseas who are possibly good enough to play in the league," he said.

This was a time when nearly all players in the NBA were American-born, and the vast majority were Black. We dominated basketball in the United States and around the globe. It would be a long time until the days of Dirk Nowitzki and Luka Doncic, and the Greek Freak, Giannis Antetokounmpo.

Basketball was one of the few things that the Black community owned. We don't own much in this country, so we don't give anything away easily.

"Coach," I said, "are you telling me there's not a player down in Alabama who is as good as the guys in Europe? You're wasting all that money flying across the globe to get some guy in Europe over there taking our jobs."

I could see in his face that the conversation had come to a halt, and a teaching moment had arrived. Coach Russell grabbed my shoulder.

"Son," he said, "as an African American, you should never disagree with inclusion."

Never again would I look at players from overseas in the same way. I would make a strong effort to avoid referring to them as European players. That insinuates that they are "less than" and that they have to be separated and evaluated apart from Americans.

I had always understood inclusion to be the foundation that Black Americans live on. Not handouts, mind you, but true inclusion. With one comment, Coach Russell made me see the hypocrisy of viewing any group as an "other." He taught me that if I was truly mindful of my heritage, I had to be inclusive to all groups.

That conversation also taught me indirectly to hate the term "Black coaches." Why make it a separate category? Let's not call John Thompson the first Black coach to win a national championship. He was the first coach at Georgetown to win.

· · ·

As the season started, our Sacramento team played poorly—and Coach Russell was not a good loser. He was honest about our performance in a way that some would call brutal.

I've noticed that athletes who have achieved greatness can, at times, take for granted how great they are. That can lead to unrealistic expectations for those who are merely good.

Once, Coach was explaining how our team wasn't rebounding well in a game. LaSalle "Tank" Thompson was our center at the time and maybe the nicest man I've ever met. You know the phrase "He would give you the shirt off his back"? I actually saw LaSalle do that for a teammate who spilled coffee on his shirt.

But LaSalle did have a habit of asking a lot of questions, and that could annoy Coach. He asked Coach Russell what he would do on a particular play to get the rebound.

"I'd just go get it," Coach said.

"But, Coach, what was your shooting percentage when you played? Wasn't it easier playing then?"

I knew this was trouble for LaSalle. My first thought was, *He's talking to possibly the best professional basketball player ever, the centerpiece of the Celtics dynasty. He's about to get a reminder of that.*

Coach Russell was never one to back down from a verbal challenge.

"My percentage was eleven out of thirteen," he said simply. "Eleven rings in thirteen years."

The room was silent. Lesson learned: Always think team, always count wins.

As the season went on, Coach's tough, suffer-no-fools approach continued. During practice, he would typically sit on the sidelines while his assistant, Willis Reed, ran the show (imagine that: your rookie year in the league and your coaches are Bill Russell and Willis Reed).

One day during a losing streak we were practicing and Coach was sitting with his newspaper open, sipping coffee. I looked over from the court to the sideline and saw that his paper was falling down. His head was dropping. Finally he slipped and jumped out of his chair. He'd been falling asleep!

Everyone just started cracking up. He looked up at us, scowling.

"If y'all weren't so damn boring," he shouted, "I wouldn't be falling asleep. Get out of practice. Y'all thrown out."

He was right, too. We *were* boring.

I will say that there was an element to our struggles that Coach didn't seem able to grasp. Everyone who makes it to the NBA is great. But there is a level of greatness where they just don't understand how us mortals operate.

Coach Russell would actually cut players in the middle of a speech: "We need to do this more or that more—and oh, by the way, Bill and Joe, go see the trainer after the meeting."

I'd look around and think, *Damn, he just cut them.*

His mindset was, if you deserve to get cut, you should know it, so getting cut in the middle of a meeting is not a big deal. He didn't understand why you would even want to be the last player on the team. Coach was callous, but in my opinion, it often benefited us. Or at least it benefited me.

We have calluses on the bottoms of our feet. You need a certain amount of them if you're a long-distance runner. You can have too many, and that hinders you. You can have too few, and that definitely hinders you. But a certain number of calluses helps you run.

One night on the road, he invited the team to his suite for a meeting, turned off the lights, and rolled game film. After that was done, Coach flipped on the lights, then glanced down at a fruit bowl on the table.

From there he looked over at Ed Pinckney, a forward who'd won a national championship at Villanova. Ed had an apple in his hand.

"Ed," Coach said. "Did you eat my fruit?"

"Y-yeah," Ed said, stammering. "I just . . ."

"Everybody out," Coach said. "You don't just come to my room and take stuff without asking. Meeting's over."

We looked at him, stunned, but he was serious.

"I have boundaries," he said. "And there are no boundaries on this team. So I'm going to hold people accountable. If you're walking in my room, ask me if you can have the fruit, or get out."

As we filed out of the suite, I said to Ed, "We just got thrown out because you ate his food."

"Yeah . . . ," Ed said, like he couldn't quite believe it.

Some of the guys were laughing, just like we did when Coach fell asleep at practice. As I looked at them, I felt more sympathetic to Coach's point of view. Boundaries *are* important. Accountability *is* important.

"Yo, you guys really *don't* have any boundaries," I said as they continued to crack up. "Y'all just taking shit."

Boundaries were important to Coach Russell in a number of contexts. It was well known that he didn't sign autographs, though I didn't know why at first.

Once we were in Hawaii for a preseason game, and Coach

picked up the check for a tableful of players. I begged the waitress to let me keep the receipt—"You don't understand; no one has Bill Russell's autograph," I said—but she wouldn't give it up.

Eventually I asked him about it. That's when he told me about the time when he was playing for the Celtics and someone wrote "nigger" on his garage door.

"I might be signing an autograph for the person who actually did that," he said. "So I'm not signing any."

That statement might read as bitter, but it didn't sound that way when he said it. He was matter-of-fact. It came across more as a simple issue of principle: *As much as I've done for the city of Boston, that I would have to come home to that—well, you know what? I have limits with you. And this is my limit. This is extra. Signing autographs is extra.*

Plus, when someone approached him for an autograph, he wasn't nasty about it.

"What's your name?" he would say.

"Kenny," the fan might say.

"Hey, Kenny," Coach would respond. "I don't sign autographs, but I appreciate you asking."

He gave his fans a moment, which was just as good. If you really wanted an interaction with Bill Russell, you got it.

·   ·   ·

Coach Russell didn't make it through that season, relieved of his on-court duties after fifty-eight games because we lacked the talent to win. He lasted another year in the front office before the organization moved on entirely from him.

This was hardly a stain on his legacy. Coach went on to collect many more accolades. In 2011, President Obama awarded him the

Presidential Medal of Freedom, the highest designation a civilian can receive in this country.

In 2013, the city of Boston—where Coach had triumphed on the court and been the victim of unspeakable racism off it—unveiled a statue of him in City Hall Plaza.

By 2020, when the George Floyd and Jacob Blake protests erupted around the country and I walked off the TNT set in solidarity, Coach Russell had long been established as a tough, unapologetic pioneer who spoke truth to power. That's why it was such a surprise and honor when he tweeted about what I did.

"I'm moved by all the @NBA players for standing up for what is right," Coach wrote that night. "To my man @TheJetOnTNT I would like to say Thank you for what you did to show your support for the players. I am so proud of you. Keep getting in good trouble."

You never know if people feel the respect for you that you feel for them. Bill Russell knew Malcolm X and Martin Luther King Jr. For him to pay attention to me in the frenzy of another civil rights movement—well, that was quite an honor.

I'll tell you what, though: those rides home more than three decades earlier were just as much of an honor.

Coach picked me as his protégé, and I'll forever be more conscious because of it.

CHAPTER FIVE

MICHAEL JACKSON
(Not the Singer!)

NO ONE DOES IT ALONE

The Bishop O'Connell Tournament in Arlington, Virginia, was a who's who of high school basketball excellence, and this year our Archbishop Molloy team was on fire—especially me.

It was January 1982, and I was a junior. I had never played as well in my young career. My basketball spider senses had kicked in, and every play I made was correct. I was leading the tournament in steals, assists, and points, and our team had made the semifinals.

While waiting to play, we went to the gym to watch some of the earlier semifinal games. Standing in the tunnel, I looked toward a section reserved for college coaches.

In walked the legendary John Thompson from Georgetown University.

At that point I didn't have any scholarship offers, but my stock was on the rise. For the first time, my natural athleticism was developing into a defined skill set. I was tearing up the tournament, setting a career high in scoring.

Surely, Coach Thompson had come to see me. Georgetown was only thirty miles away from the tournament site, and he must have heard what I was doing.

Our game was up next. I began stretching with my teammates off to the side of the court. I was ready to put on a show for this coach. There was no way the great John Thompson was going to walk out of that gym without raving to his staff about the kid from Queens, Kenny Smith.

"I need him to be a Hoya," he would say.

I looked over at my two best friends on the team, George Kingland and Chris Sterling.

"Man, Chris, Kenny brought John Thompson out!" George screamed.

"Yep," I said. "You better know it! Let's get busy!"

The crowd roared as Coach Thompson entered the gym. He moved with the grace of a king. He was it!

For an inner-city basketball player, Georgetown was the epitome of greatness. It was where basketball met hip-hop met Muhammad Ali. I didn't watch much college basketball at that time, being a Knicks and NBA fan—but I did follow Georgetown. Coach Thompson and his program had a cultural relevance that went beyond the sport.

He was anti-establishment. They didn't give him respect; he took it. He was an unapologetic Black man with attitude. Georgetown offered a great education and had a top basketball team. But most important, it had Coach Thompson.

Rap music and Georgetown, that was me. I had the gray and blue Hoya sneakers with the jacket to match.

As Thompson and his staff walked in, he stopped to hug one of the players in the current game, the starting point guard from South Lakes High School in Virginia.

Who was that guy? Then I heard it over the loudspeaker.

"Congratulations to point guard Michael Jackson, new signee for the Georgetown Hoyas!" the announcer said. "Yes, Michael Jackson from South Lakes, not the singer!"

My heart broke. Michael Jackson? A dude named after the singer? Come on, man. That's my spot!

I vowed to make the championship game to play against this Michael Jackson and show Coach Thompson he had the wrong guy. I was the one he wanted.

We did take that semifinal game and go on to win the championship. I was named tournament MVP. But my plan didn't work. Michael's team lost in the semis and Coach didn't stick around to see me play. I hated Michael for that.

He was a year ahead of me. He went on to play at Georgetown, and I ended up at the University of North Carolina. I was happy there, and Coach Dean Smith became one of the great mentors of my life. But that didn't mean I resented Michael Jackson any less.

What made matters worse was that Coach Thompson and Coach Smith were friends, sharing a great mutual affinity and respect. Coach Smith would often compare our practices or my play to Georgetown and their point guard.

"Oh, you couldn't do this if you were at Georgetown," he would say. "You couldn't get away with that if you were at Georgetown."

Meanwhile, I played great in college. I started to think I was better than anybody—and Coach Smith was still comparing me to Michael Jackson. When I watched Michael win the NCAA championship his junior year, I hated him even more. I had never met the guy. I had no idea if he was a good guy or not, and I didn't care.

After my senior year, *Basketball Times* magazine voted me college player of the year. I was a consensus first-team All-American, and Bill Russell made me the sixth overall pick for his Sacramento Kings in the 1987 NBA draft.

After a three-week holdout, I agreed to a contract and flew to California to join the team and launch my pro career.

Upon landing, I was greeted by adoring fans and team executives. Julie Fie, long one of the best PR people in the business, guided me from interview to interview and then to a news conference. After all the excitement I headed straight to training camp.

There, a staff member asked if I wanted a single or double room. A single meant paying extra for privacy. If you chose to have a roommate, the team paid (I sometimes imagine how it would play out today if teams tried to make players pay for a single room in the present era . . . but I digress).

I was young, Black, and single in a city that felt like a small town. I knew no one. It wasn't hard to decide on the double room with a roommate.

Excited for the start of my lifelong dream, I hurried through the hotel lobby and into the elevator with the bellman and my bags.

As I opened the door to my room I heard, "Wassup, Kenny!"

Oh my god. It was Michael Jackson. They were gonna make me room with this dude?

This might sound hard to believe, but I didn't even know Michael was on the team. He'd signed as a free agent a few weeks earlier, but I had delusions of grandeur at that age.

I'm in town, I'd thought. *Who cares who else is here?*

Plus, when I was holding out I'd made a conscious decision not to pay attention to what Sacramento was doing. That would have made me antsy to play, thereby weakening my resolve. And now I was there with my archnemesis.

"I'm so happy you're here," Michael said.

I responded with a lukewarm nod of the head and a cold "Wassup."

Something was suspicious. This was a guy whom I had never met, and who had probably heard that same stuff about me from Coach Thompson that I'd heard about him from Coach Smith.

And he seemed genuinely happy I was there, even though my presence probably meant he would never play. What kind of trickery was going on here?

I'm from the streets of New York. I know a setup when I see one. This dude was trying to soften me up for the kill.

But no, it wasn't anything like that. As I discovered almost immediately, this was Michael, as a Black man, having a full understanding that for the two of us to be divided would hurt the entire community.

Black people can fall into the trap of feeling competitive with one another because of a fear or awareness that "they"—white America—are only going to allow a certain number of us to be successful.

This is rooted in the trauma and fear passed down through generations. For many Black people, particularly our ancestors, this has indeed been the case.

Think of this analogy: Black Americans live in a bottle. The bottle represents the hardships on the path to success. As we all try to move up, we face a bottleneck that prevents us from getting out.

We are poured out at the slow pace of a new bottle of ketchup. Some of us will make it out, and some of us won't. If you are born at the back of the bottle—maybe because of a poor or broken family, a bad education system, or systemic racism, police brutality, and racist ignorance—you might not make it out no matter how hard you work. It's impossible to push through all those people. There are also people who try to hold you back or step on you to reach certain heights.

Some of us are born at the front of the bottle. Maybe we have affluent parents or access to health care and great school systems. We may be athletically gifted or have a God-given singing voice that the world wants to hear. Our culture values those skills, so it puts us at the front of the bottle toward white America.

The mentality in the bottle of hardship can be "Don't share, don't cheer, stand clear."

The people who make it out often forget to reach back and help those still in—hence the saying "You forgot where you came from."

Can you honestly fully blame them, though? After they've

clawed, scraped, been humiliated, thought of as "less than," and even pulled back by other Black people, should their first thought be to help those still inside the bottle?

It takes a very special individual to do that. The energy it takes to make it out can knock you unconscious. But the ones who do remember, we call them "woke" and "conscious thinkers." This is an obligation and burden that, in my eyes, only Black Americans bear.

No other racial group is asked, "What have you done for your people? What have you provided for your neighborhood that you've ascended from?"

There was a song that my mom played in our home every Sunday morning by James Cleveland, "I Don't Feel No Ways Tired." Well, we as Black Americans are not allowed to be tired.

As I sat and listened to Michael Jackson welcome me, I decided to let my guard down.

"Yo, man, let me tell you about the team," he said. "Here's our plays, so you can jump right in and be ready tomorrow."

He talked about the tendencies of our players and provided many other insights intended to make me better, even though that would mean less playing time for him. The guy I hated was not a hater. He was giving me directions to be successful, to get out of the bottle. Michael wanted to share and empower.

At twenty-one years old, I had never seen that—especially growing up in NYC, and especially in sports. This is a job in which you compete to make not only your opponents yield to submission, but also your teammates. It's a cutthroat business.

While on the court, Michael could be as tough and ruthless as anyone—you had to have that quality to survive in the NBA—but he had a switch that he could turn off when the game ended.

When I landed in Sacramento, I didn't have that switch. I wasn't going to give information to the competition, internal or external. From Michael, I learned to be more inclusive and generous. It started that first night, when we clicked immediately.

Superficially, we didn't have much in common. He was a clean-cut guy, an intellectual who wasn't into hip-hop music and hip-hop style like I was.

But we fell into an easy rhythm as we compared notes about Georgetown and North Carolina and learned that Coach Smith and Coach Thompson used the same comparisons to motivate us. I told stories about Michael Jordan, and he filled me in on what it had been like to play with Patrick Ewing.

Before long, we expanded our conversation to bigger ideas. Michael was what we then called a "militant" and would now call "conscious."

He was always thinking about why Black people did things. "Here's why you wear gold chains," he would say, or "Here's why you wear your hair that way."

This is why I called him Chip: it was like he always had a chip on his shoulder, or so it seemed to me at the time. Now I see that he was actually just aware.

Michael not only spoke his mind, but he was also an information guru on Black history. He taught me where slave ships first landed and about Madam C. J. Walker, the first Black woman entrepreneur to become a millionaire in America.

He understood the importance of fighting for ourselves financially. "Don't let them do you any kind of way, Kenny!" he would say.

Michael described to me a plan for his future that revolved around first using his athletic talents to attain a level of financial security, and then launching his long-term career in business. He was self-aware about his abilities and limitations.

"I'm only going to play until I get my pension, and then I'm done," he told me. "I'm not going to be a guy who's going to be able to play ten or twelve years in the NBA."

"What?" I said. "Come on, Michael, you're not going to try to play longer than that?"

"I gotta get my three years in," he said. "I gotta get that pension. I'm not good enough to last much longer. Give me that pension and then I'm gone. I'm good."

Not long after, Michael almost lost that opportunity. To this day, I don't think he knows the story.

Coach Russell always called me into his office to talk about the game plan for the night. He and I had hit it off immediately, so our conversations were friendly and relaxed.

"Oh, by the way," he said as I was leaving his office one day. "I'm gonna have to cut your buddy from the team today."

"Michael?" I asked.

"Yes," he said. "If we keep him past today, we have to pay him for the entire year."

My heart dropped. I knew that Michael had more passion for the game than any of the other players remaining on that sorry Sacramento team. I couldn't let my guy get the axe. Or, as Michael would have put it, I couldn't let them do him like that.

"Coach," I said, "can I give the difference of my salary for him to stay?"

Coach looked at me, puzzled. "You would go to bat for him like that?"

"Yes," I said firmly. "He's a winner, Coach. You've got a handful of guys who don't even care if we win. You've said it yourself to me. They get to stay and we send a winner home? That's crazy to me."

Coach Russell paused to think for a moment. "Well, Kenny," he finally said, "the NBA's collective bargaining agreement won't allow me to do that. But since you went to bat for him, we will keep him."

I was overjoyed. I've never told Michael that story and still feel that he stayed on merit, not just because of me. Bill Russell wasn't going to carry a player on his roster just because that player was a friend of mine.

I tell the story now not to pat myself on the back, but to show what I learned from Michael, and how quickly I learned it: when I saw something, I spoke up.

Michael's lesson about advocating for those who can't be heard continues to drive me, now on a much bigger stage. A squeaky wheel will get oiled.

Trayvon Martin, Breonna Taylor, George Floyd, and countless others need someone to speak for them. Taking small stands can have a huge impact on another person's life.

And no one does it alone. At that time, Michael needed someone to speak up for him, and I did. That helped him get into a position to one day do the same for me.

Over the next few years, Michael's plan worked perfectly. Just as he predicted, he lasted three years in the NBA. Upon retiring, he took a job at the U.S. Olympic Committee and started climbing a corporate ladder that would ultimately lead him to Turner Sports and Nike.

By the mid-1990s he was a top executive at Turner. Every year, TNT would bring in players to analyze games with Ernie Johnson. Michael would always invite me in if the Houston Rockets had an early exit from the playoffs.

I had a leg up, because my wife at the time, Dawn, was a news anchor in Little Rock, Arkansas. We would often sit up at night and talk about what would make her better. My job was to tape her episodes and critique them. Now she was explaining to me how a live studio show is made.

By the time I began appearing on TNT, I was able to apply the knowledge that Dawn gave me. This impressed the producers, but initially, I was just mimicking her skills. It was fun, but it never seemed like a second career to me.

One of the producers, Tim Kiely, was particularly complimentary. "Kenny, you could be a star at this TV gig if you want," he would say.

Honestly, I thought he fed that line to everyone who came on the show. But TK meant it. All these years later he still runs our show, and I'm forever grateful for the early encouragement.

At the time, though, I really just wanted to come in, shoot the breeze with my friend Michael for a couple days, and get out of there.

Prior to the 1997–98 NBA season, I was thinking of retiring. My career had entered a different phase. The previous season, I had bounced between Detroit, Orlando, and Denver. I could hang on as a journeyman, but I wasn't sure I wanted to.

TK called and suggested that this was the time to focus on a job in television. There was an opportunity at TNT, and I would be strongly in the mix if I decided to pursue it.

Unwilling to totally cut the cord on my athletic career, I decided to accept an invitation from the New Jersey Nets to try to make their team. It might seem odd from the outside that an athlete accustomed to starting and winning championships would be willing to accept a part-time role, and even the risk of getting cut. But truthfully, it wasn't difficult to be in that stage of my career, because I didn't think of it like that.

Athletes have to be delusional until the end. You don't think, *I hope I make the team.* You think, *They'd do well to understand that they need me.*

I called Michael and told him I was going to give it one more shot. He didn't think it was the right move.

"These TV jobs don't open up all the time," he said. "You should think twice."

Turner was considering just two candidates: me and Bob Hill, who had just been fired as head coach of the San Antonio Spurs.

Michael made it sound like I would be the front-runner, if only I wanted it. He said that everyone thought I could be a success in the TV game. But basketball was my first love. I didn't dream of talking about the sport, I dreamed of playing it.

The Nets wanted me to be a backup point guard for the first time in my career, behind my ex-teammate Sam Cassell. Sam had been my backup on the championship Rockets teams.

The Nets were up-and-coming and had a charismatic leader in John Calipari. I loved his energy and his ability to get the most out of talent. He was a coach about to make his mark.

Training camp was going great, with young, talented players Keith Van Horn, Kendall Gill, Kerry Kittles, and Jayson Williams, a rebounding machine. In later years, this would be the core that would reach the NBA Finals with Jason Kidd and Kenyon Martin.

I hung out with Sam and Jayson, who was a fellow Queens native and a former St. John's University star. He was the most original guy I had ever met, with perhaps the widest array of interests I had seen in a Black guy from NYC.

He would listen to rap music one minute and rock and roll the next. He would be at the opera and then want to go to the Florida Everglades and see crocodiles. He had friends who dressed hip-hop and friends who looked like mob gangsters. Friends in three-piece suits and in tracksuits.

Everyone loved Jayson. He had a quick wit and humor that were very similar to those of my current TV partner, Charles Barkley. Jayson would have the entire bus laughing after games.

One day after practice Jayson came racing into the locker room, screaming, "Where's Kenny?"

Then he grabbed me and said, "We've gotta talk! Are you thinking about doing TV at TNT?"

"Yeah," I said, wondering where he was going with this.

"Take the job!" he said.

Jayson had just been in the training room, where he'd overheard Coach Calipari talking on the phone with his buddy, Bob Hill— the other candidate for the Turner gig.

"He said he's going to keep you here until the start of the season, so Bob can get the job," Jayson told me. "Then he's going to cut you from the team."

My heart sank. For the first time, it felt like the game I loved so much wasn't loving me back.

Part of me didn't believe Jayson. First of all, he was a jokester. Second, I didn't know Calipari well enough to believe he would or wouldn't do that. I certainly wanted to believe that he would not.

I decided in the short term to file it away and work harder to prove everyone wrong. Even if Coach Cal was working behind my back to undermine me like that, I would show my worth to the Nets and make it impossible for him to cut me.

Two days before opening night, the Nets released me and signed Sherman Douglas. Bob Hill signed with TNT. I spent a week contemplating my next career move. Other teams were calling, and I had an offer to play in Italy.

I've always joked that I get rid of the things that don't want me anyway—friends, relationships, even my hair. My hair was thinning, so I shaved it off first.

Now, while there were still some opportunities, the game of basketball was closer to rejecting me than it had ever been before. I knew I'd arrived at a crucial crossroads in my life.

I prayed at night with a different sense of purpose. I prayed to be rid of everything that wasn't supposed to be in my life.

One day while I was driving, I prayed and said, "I'm only going to listen, God. No more words."

I started to hear a phrase, first one time and then repeatedly.

"Twenty-four hours," a voice said. "Twenty-four hours."

I actually turned around and looked at the back seat, thinking someone was there. Without yet knowing what the phrase meant, I realized that I was having one of those special moments of clarity.

It happens every once in a while, usually when I'm not asking for something. *I'm just gonna sit here and listen,* I'll think. And then, every now and then, I'll hear.

This time, the message was audible, but its meaning was vague. Twenty-four hours? Finally I realized: I was going to make a major career decision within twenty-four hours.

The next morning I called Michael to gauge his temperature.

"Hey, I'm thinking I want to do TV," I said.

He laughed.

"You know we just signed Bob Hill," he said. "But OK, jump on a plane to Atlanta. I have to look in your eyes."

I flew to Atlanta the next day and sat in Michael's office as an array of TNT talent cycled through to say hello: Kevin Harlan, Cheryl Miller, Ernie Johnson. And Bob Hill. Michael and I fell into our old rhythm, talking about games, teams, and players as we always did.

Then he stopped, cut me off, and said, "What did you do about the situation with Calipari and Bob Hill? Did you confront Calipari?"

I was shocked.

"You heard about that?" I said.

"Yeah, some reporter from the *New York Post* asked me about it a couple weeks ago," he said. "Right in the middle of me negotiating Bob's contract. I had no idea if it was true or not—but if it was true, I couldn't let them do my boy Kenny like that. So I spoke up for you."

It was our old line, with yet another twist.

"How?" I said.

"After that rumor, I signed Bob to a month-to-month contract with a six-month guarantee, so if you became available, I could sign you," he said. "If you want the job in six months, it's yours. But you can't hoop anymore. You gotta be serious about TV. I gotta know you're finished, or I'm gonna sign him for the rest of the year and offer a multiyear deal."

I thought about that first night hanging out with Michael, when I got past my resentment and quickly came to admire his intelligence and judgment. Then I thought about fighting for him when he didn't know. And about him fighting for me when I didn't know.

I looked up at him.

"I'm done playing," I said. "I'll be here in six months."

As for the situation with John Calipari, I've obviously seen him multiple times since then, and neither one of us has ever talked about or mentioned the episode. Regardless of rumor, innuendo, or truth, life continues. We—or maybe I—have gone past it . . . to the point that if I had a son who was good enough to play for him at Kentucky, I would encourage it.

CHAPTER SIX

CHARLES BARKLEY

FROM MALCOLM X TO UNCLE TOM . . . IN THE SAME NIGHT

Filmed in grainy black and white, looking right into the camera in close-up, Charles Barkley utters the words that would come to define him for much of his playing career and beyond:

> *I am not a role model. I'm not paid to be a role model. I'm paid to wreak havoc on the basketball court. Parents should be role models. Just because I dunk a basketball doesn't mean I should raise your kids.*

My first significant impression of Chuck—the one-of-a-kind man who later became my co-analyst, sparring partner on politics and social issues, teammate, and brother—was probably the same as yours: that iconic Nike ad in 1993.

If Michael Jordan's commercials of that era were blockbusters, this was an artsy independent film, with more complicated themes, touching on Chuck's beliefs about sports, families, and society.

The spot became the subject of much discussion about the role of star athletes. Charles was nearly as famous for it as for his MVP campaign that year for the Phoenix Suns.

Those brief thirty seconds captured the complexity of Charles Barkley: he was making a point that was ultimately positive, but doing it in a way that came across on the surface as negative, at least if you weren't paying close attention.

His words, and the commercial's stark presentation of them, gave the viewer an initial jolt. If you got past that jolt, you heard his real message, which was that mothers and fathers were the true role models. It was actually a compliment to the people raising us.

But because his tone was so pointed, most people looked at it and said, "How could you not want to be a role model?" They saw it as a negative.

Simply put, my friend Chuck is the king of mixed messages.

Sitting next to him for two decades at the *Inside the NBA* desk, I've often watched him make a sharp point about social justice, like how the lack of education in the inner city leads to inequalities.

And then, in the same breath, he will pivot to a comment more aligned with conservative thought, like, "Because your moms and dads don't take you to school."

He'll go from being Malcolm X to people calling him Uncle Tom—in the same night.

It used to be confusing to me, but it isn't confusing anymore. There is always a backstory to what he's saying. It's informed by his own experience and sharpened by his continued thought and study.

Make no mistake: just because I understand where Chuck is coming from doesn't mean we agree often. Because we air out our differences on the show, people assume that this means we don't like each other.

Strangers will come up to me on the street, ready to commiserate about how terrible he is and assuming that I'll be on their side.

"Whoa, whoa, whoa," I'll say. "You can't talk to me like that about him. That's my guy."

Put it this way: Chuck might be a butthole, but he's my butthole.

And on a more serious note, please understand that he is as responsible as anyone for the voice that I have—and the voice that so many NBA players now enjoy. The fact that Chuck and I are on different sides of the fence on specific topics doesn't do anything to change this.

In an era of renewed athlete activism, this is a crucially important point. In the twenty-five years before Charles came along, there was virtually no voice in sports. After Muhammad Ali left the stage, there was no athlete to whom reporters and fans could turn to discuss an issue other than how many points we scored.

As a player in the 1980s, I would have been happy to talk about what I saw happening in the country and across the world. I was right there in the locker room, and reporters were there, too. But no one would ask me.

Charles was one of the only athletes during those years who sought it out. As the reporters asked game-related questions, he would bring other issues into the conversation. *Did you hear about what's in the news?* he would say.

By forcing the issue, he eventually became the sports figure whom reporters would ask about off-the-court situations. After a while they wouldn't even ask him a basketball question. Chuck was brash and charismatic like Ali, though certainly their politics didn't always align. He did inherit Ali's role as the athlete who was invited by reporters to speak out about off-the-court issues.

Watching that from afar, I thought, *Oh, man, no one ever asks me those questions.*

It's not easy to be that go-to guy in a locker room to talk about world events. You just played a forty-eight-minute game. Your knees are on fire. Your ankles are throbbing; your back is hurting. You're trying to get iced up and out of that locker room.

It takes a special person to take that on. When Charles did it, he laid the groundwork for LeBron James refusing to shut up and dribble.

He laid the groundwork for Chris Paul's work with historically Black colleges and universities, and then Harvard Business School.

His engagement as a player kept alive the spirit that later sent Carmelo Anthony out marching in the streets to protest police violence against Black people. It laid the groundwork for LeBron James's outspokenness.

And then when Chuck retired from the court and brought it to television, he poured kerosene on the flame he'd lit during his playing career. Now, instead of providing a sound bite, he had a voice.

If it weren't for him I wouldn't have the voice that I'm using even now, writing this book. Before I arrived at Turner, they had a solid basketball show. I'd like to think that I helped to turn it into a great basketball show. But Chuck made it a great TV show.

By demanding for himself a voice on social issues, he helped me to find that voice, too. Now, because of Chuck, people finally ask me the questions I wanted to be asked all along. I'm forever grateful to him for this.

I love the guy, but that doesn't mean it's easy. Quite the contrary. With Charles Barkley, it's always complicated.

.   .   .

Charles and I played against each other in the league for years, including an epic Eastern Conference Semifinals in 1995, when my Rockets came within seconds of losing to his Suns in game seven.

That game featured what was probably the most famous shot in the history of the Rockets franchise, Mario Elie's tiebreaking three-pointer with ten seconds remaining. Mario followed the shot by blowing a kiss at the Phoenix bench, a moment forever known as the "Kiss of Death."

It was a tremendous series, but Chuck and I were merely competitors and did not know each other personally.

At the beginning of a jump ball we would shake hands, and that was it, other than his constant trash talk throughout the game.

I recognized him as a great player, but thought our teams had better players than theirs and was always confident we would beat them.

The Suns played at a fast pace that worked for us, because it enabled me, Sam Cassell, Vernon Maxwell, and Mario to get more opportunities. Growing up in New York, that's the way I played: up and down, up and down. There was no setup. It's streetball.

The Suns had more of a streetball style, so I loved playing them. I felt that in a seven-game series against Phoenix, I was sure to have at least three really good games.

Kevin Johnson was great and so was Charles, but we had better all-around athletes. And sure enough, we edged them in those conference semis, despite their superior record during the regular season. We were on our way to a second consecutive NBA championship.

My introduction to Charles on a more human level came the following season, during a challenging time for me professionally.

After enjoying so much success over the previous two seasons, I found myself in a five- or six-game stretch in which I did not play well. Our head coach, Rudy Tomjanovich, called me into his office.

Rudy and I had a different relationship than what I'd enjoyed with other coaches like Dean Smith and Bill Russell. Those two had forged close bonds with me that included, as the starting point guard, time in their offices discussing pregame strategy and life in general.

Rudy never really talked to me on a personal level. This was the first time in, like, six years that I had even been in his office. I was looking around at the pictures on his walls and thinking, *This is not going to be good news.*

"I'm going to take you out of the lineup," he said. "I think I'm going to start Cassell."

"All right," I said, standing up. "It's your choice, Rudy. You're the coach."

But later, when he told Sam that he was promoting him from backup to starter, Sam declined.

"What do you mean you're not going to start?" Rudy said.

"Because I know that by the time we get to the playoffs, Kenny is going to be playing well enough where he's going to be starting again," Sam said. "And I don't want to be in and out. I like my role coming off the bench. I play with the second unit. I get all the shots."

Now Rudy was in a bind. Having benched me and been turned down by Sam, he decided he was going to start Eldridge Recasner, the third-string guard. Eldridge had spent most of his pro career in the Continental Basketball Association and had not been playing that season.

I suddenly became the third-string guard. I had two or three games where I didn't even play. It was a quick fall from champion to DNP, but I tried to stay ready and be a good teammate.

During this stretch of games, I invited my dad to come to practice. After the rest of the team finished, he came on the court to rebound while I shot. It was an attempt to get back to the basics of what got me there. I knew I was eventually going to play again, whether it was for the Rockets or someone else.

That day, Eldridge was working out alone on the other end of the court. He had never been a starter. Now he was trying to go from not playing to going at John Stockton, Kevin Johnson, and Gary Payton. Good luck.

Eldridge, through no fault of his, had been put in a tough position, and he was struggling. I looked down the court and saw him working on a pick and roll—and doing it 100 percent wrong. I couldn't take it. I had to go help the guy.

"Eldridge, man, here's some things I see," I said, walking toward him.

When I shared my insight with him, it was like a light went on.

"Oh, whoa!" he said, beginning to see the game differently.

Back down on the other end of the court, my dad yelled at me.

"What the hell did you do that for?" he said, aghast that I would help the guy who took my job.

"Dad, at the end of the day I'm on the team," I said. "I can't let him struggle. Even though he's taking my spot, I'm gonna give him my information."

Unbeknownst to me, a reporter was also watching and wrote a nice article about it.

A few more games passed, and I collected a few more DNPs. Trying to stay in game shape, I would arrive at the arena three hours early to run sprints, although I went at it so hard that by game time I'd be gassed and yawning on the sidelines.

When we played the Bulls, Scottie Pippen became the first opponent to speak up, telling the press that he didn't understand how I could go from being a starter on a championship team to not playing.

Before our game against Phoenix, I was on the layup line when I heard my name.

"Hey, Kenny!" someone shouted. "Smith!"

I looked around. It was a loud arena, and I couldn't tell who was calling me. Then I saw Charles gesturing toward me.

"Come here!" he said.

We moved toward each other. I had never talked to Charles in my life.

"Hey, man, I want to tell you something," he said. "I love the way you're handling this situation. You're a pro. That's what pros do. You could be over there bitching and moaning, and you're over there helping your teammates. You're helping Rudy out. You're a pro."

Then he gave me a playful shove onto the sideline. That ensured that everyone on my team would know that we'd had the interaction. Vernon Maxwell looked at me as if to say, *You know Charles like that?*

I downplayed it, but they still eyed me funny, clearly wondering why Charles Barkley was in the middle of our layup line. The moment stuck with me. That was the first time that I regarded Chuck as different.

Anyone could have said what he said in the papers. Anyone could have said it on TV. But to physically come over and let me know that he was paying attention to what I was doing—well, that was a little different.

It also gave me a boost of confidence to hear that I was in fact handling this situation the right way. The guys who were the greatest in the league were looking at it and going, *He's doing it right.* I thought so, but it's always good to have people like that in your corner.

Now, for a glimpse at the complexity of Charles, let's flash forward about twenty years. We were shooting a roundtable show for NBA TV in which Charles, Isiah Thomas, and I told old NBA stories.

The situation with my benching came up, and I revealed how Charles had gone out of his way to support me. I told him that I appreciated it. He looked at me blankly.

"I said that to you?" he said.

Yeah, Chuck. Thanks for remembering.

.   .   .

When I joined TNT in 1998, they had a pretty good basketball show. ESPN was the dominant network, and we were low profile by comparison.

As a viewer, I enjoyed the sense of calm that Ernie Johnson

brought as host. It was a welcome alternative to the shouting, over-the-top style of ESPN.

Upon my arrival, I had a lot to learn about broadcasting—but to the everlasting credit of Ernie and our longtime producer, Tim Kiely, they were open to my ideas about style and presentation. The network wanted me to wear white shirts, because that's what newscasters did.

"I don't want to wear white shirts," I said. "Why do I have to look like that?"

"OK," TK said. "Wear what you want."

So I chose outfits that felt more natural to me, as a thirty-six-year-old guy just out of the league. I wore designer shirts and cool shoes. That wasn't the only tweak that I requested to make the show feel more natural. At first they instructed me to look at the camera while answering a question, rather than at the person who asked it.

Out of the corner of my eye, I would glimpse Ernie looking at his notes and getting ready for his next comment. But if I was telling a joke—or making a serious point, for that matter—I wanted to see his reaction. How else would I know if it was working?

"I don't want to talk to the camera anymore," I told TK.

"Don't talk to the camera, then," he said. "We have ten cameras in the studio. We'll find you."

When Chuck arrived, he told me that those elements attracted him to the show. Very early on, I came to understand the power that he could wield. Before Chuck, the show was Ernie, me, and Peter Vecsey, who would join about once a week.

Peter was a longtime NBA columnist for the *New York Post* and a big presence around the game. I'd grown up reading him, but later came to understand that his methods were not always above-board. Once during my playing career, he called me after I'd been traded.

"Hey, I'm just looking for some quotes on how you feel about the trade," he said.

"Pete, I love your column," I said. "I'm happy to talk to you."

We discussed the trade for a few minutes, and then he said, "So tell me about the drugs."

I was stunned.

"The drugs?"

"Yeah," he said. "There have been some rumors that you're late for practice, and there could possibly be some drug use."

"Whoa, Pete," I said. "I don't even drink alcohol. I'm thirty years old and I've never even had a beer. I can't imagine who would say that about me."

"Yeah, no one said that," he confessed. "I was just seeing if it would stick."

From then on I called him Messy Vecsey. I loved him because his column was entertaining, but I understood who he was.

Later on he would bring his son to my basketball camp and pose for pictures with me. It's like I said earlier about Chuck: Messy Vecsey was a butthole, but he was my butthole.

But Chuck didn't like him at all. Peter had criticized him in his columns and did it on air, too. Chuck was like, *He's a butthole and he's not my butthole.*

It was bumpy at first, because when the two would argue, I would take the side of whoever I thought was right. That was new for Chuck. I didn't do alliances; I just landed on the side of what I thought in a given situation.

Before long it got to the point where it was going to be Chuck or Peter. Chuck was like, *I'm not gonna be here if this dude is here.* And they got rid of Pete.

That wasn't the only early example of Charles's influence. You could see it around the studio in more subtle ways. When he first arrived at TNT, everyone would kiss his ass. It was like, *Oh my god, Charles Barkley is here.* That bothered the hell out of me. It was just too much. They'd laugh at his every joke. They'd suck up to him.

On the one hand, Chuck was great to the staff and crew. He'd invite everyone for drinks and buy the entire bar out. He would bring flowers to all the women and buy them pedicures.

No one wanted to mess that up, so they looked the other way when he was rude or abrasive. He's the kind of guy who, if he sees a man with a limp, he'll say, "What's up, Hopalong?"

Sometimes it's funny, and sometimes it's not. I was the only one who would push back.

"Oh no, you're not talking that way to me," I'd say when he tried to trash talk me.

Everyone would go, "Oooooh," like we had some kind of rivalry. I didn't love being in that position.

Other times, we would be in the greenroom around members of the crew and he'd blurt out, "Man, I just blew seven hundred thousand dollars last week in Vegas. I lost at the blackjack table."

I would have to pull him aside and say, "I think that's a little insensitive. Some of these people haven't made seven hundred thousand dollars in their life." Instead of apologizing, he would shout something like, "Well, I think they're being too sensitive because I have money."

For a while, I searched for a way to use his energy to our mutual advantage. At the outset, being from New York helped me to deal with him. New Yorkers are rude and abrasive and tell it like it is. That's how my friends were growing up.

Even though Chuck is from Alabama, he's another version of the guy in LeFrak City, Queens, who would yell at me to turn my music down while he blasted his. Because of that, I knew how to engage.

I also knew that he was talented and sensed that we could win championships together on that show. I just had to figure out how to make it work. Somewhere around our third or fourth broadcast together, it hit me: I would be his setup guy. I'm a point guard after all. I'd tee him up on jokes or insights, and he'd take the shot.

That helped us to develop a sense of trust and friendship—a sense that had its strongest early test two years later, when we strongly disagreed about a *Sports Illustrated* cover.

In 2002, *SI* somehow talked him into dressing as a slave, depicted as breaking free from chains. The headline read, "Charles Unchained: Living Large and Holding Forth on Everything from His Golf, Money and Politics to Michael Jordan, TV Sports and Enron."

I was immediately turned off by the imagery—and I was not alone. Controversy over the cover spread like wildfire, going viral before viral was a thing. It just didn't seem appropriate for Chuck to equate his own struggles in any way to an issue as serious as slavery.

He had shown poor judgment, but the cover wasn't all his fault. There must have been a whole group of people in a meeting at *SI* who approved it. There was a photographer who agreed to shoot the image. There was a wardrobe person, and someone who put the chains on.

None of those people thought to say, "Wait a minute, this might be a bad idea"? Really?

I was just as mad at all those people as I was at Chuck. And my anger toward Chuck came from a place of respect. He was better than that.

We decided to discuss it on the show.

"That shows a slave mentality there, maybe even the N-word," I told him on the air. "When were you ever chained? You've never been held back from expressing your opinions."

We didn't come to an agreement on that one but continued to

build trust and brotherhood as partners on the show. I did hold on to certain feelings about the *SI* incident, though, and finally expressed them in 2014, near the beginning of our current civil rights era.

In August of that year, Michael Brown, an eighteen-year-old Black man in Ferguson, Missouri, was shot and killed by a white police officer, Darren Wilson. In November, a grand jury decided against indicting Wilson.

This set off a round of social unrest that had deep roots in the systemic oppression of Black people. The folks who took to the streets, some of whom decided to loot stores, were angry about Brown—but they were also angry about many years of mistreatment and inequality.

When Chuck appeared on a Philadelphia radio station and was asked about the demonstrations, his comments reflected none of that perspective.

"Them jackasses who are looting," he said. "Those aren't real Black people, those are scumbags. The real Black people, they're not out there looting. I just watched on CNN where a bunch of folks, really amazing folks wouldn't let them burn down an establishment. It was a great story . . .

"There's a perception among some Black people that if you're not a thug or hood rat or if you don't wear your pants around by your ass, you're not Black enough. They're always holding us back, plain and simple."

I thought those comments were inappropriate because he didn't really remember who he was talking to. You call someone a "scumbag" and you're forgetting about that person's mom or dad who loves them and worked so hard to raise them.

When I see in the news a report of police violence against a Black person, it hits me like a death in the family. It's visceral. And while I obviously don't approve of looting or violence, I felt that

Chuck was not trying to understand the anger that can lead to a destructive choice. Instead he was calling people scumbags, which wasn't helpful. He was looking at the looting through the narrow perspective of a flashlight, when a floodlight was needed to see the big picture.

The more I thought about it, the more I had a real issue with what Chuck said. I called him.

"We're attached right now because of the show, so when you say something, I get asked about it," I said. "I'm going to do something a little different this time, because I don't want to speak about it over and over to eighteen different news stations. I'm going to write an open letter to you, so I can just tell people, 'Look at the letter.'"

"All right," he said, clearly unhappy that I was challenging him.

Ultimately, Chuck respects and even enjoys when you stare him down and stick to your guns. But he makes it tough at first. It could be a day before it becomes comfortable with him again—or it could be a week or a year. You're going to be uncomfortable for a while.

When you challenge Chuck, he puts you in a place where you think, *When this is over we're either going to be best friends, or we're never going to speak again.*

I should emphasize that, for two decades, it has always ended up being the former. Every important event that has happened in my life over the past twenty years—childbirth, deaths in the family, divorce—we've had long, deep conversations about. He calls and texts me so much that my ex-wife used to joke that she wasn't sure if I was married to her or Chuck.

Bottom line, I know where I stand with Chuck and he knows where he stands with me. But you have to walk through fire to get there.

The events in Ferguson put us in that place once again. I wrote the letter and sent it to *USA Today.* It read:

Dear Chuck,

I hope this finds you in the way I always see you, in great spirits, with great joy and full of life. There are some things I want to openly say to you that sometimes in conversation get lost.

Firstly I lied! You ARE the greatest Power Forward of all time. It's not (Tim) Duncan or (Karl) Malone, they had size and height that you weren't blessed with and you never had near the talent around you that they were blessed to have. Contrarily you took your teams to similar heights. Secondly, you are a champion in my book. Effort and determination is what makes a champion, not a ring.

Lastly, you are the most entertaining person in sports television (partly because I throw you so many assists lol).

However, what I consistently find interesting is how writers and media members view your insights in politics, and now race relations, with the same reverence as your insights in sports.

They did it in the Trayvon Martin trial and now with Mike Brown and the decision in Ferguson. It's not that you shouldn't ever have an opinion, but you are often quoted alongside the likes of Al Sharpton and even President Obama. I would hope that Sharpton or President Obama would never be referenced with you when picking the next NBA Champs!

The body of work that our Black Civil Rights leaders put in by planning, executing and activating does not justify you being in the conversation. While your body of work on the court very few compare to nor should be mentioned when you are giving your expert analysis. Again, I respect that you have an opinion on Ferguson. And here's mine.

The question must be asked: Why is there so much distrust in the police and the legal system from the African American community? Without manifesting what the effects of slavery still have today, Dec 1st still marks only 59 years since Rosa Parks sat on that memorable bus. Many of our parents and grandparents have lived through those times and have passed those stories on to all of us. Those civil rights changes were at one time the law! They were not illegal.

So did the protection of the law by the courts and police make it right? Obviously not, so as African Americans we still know and feel that there are laws and jurisdictions that severely penalize the poor and, most importantly, African Americans greater than any other group. Some laws were initially made without us as equals in mind; that's just the facts. So the thought process that it's not for us or by us will unfortunately lead to distrust.

When someone is in "the struggle," which many of our black communities are in, they are living with a lack of educational facilities, high unemployment and poor recreational facilities. The masses involved in "the struggle" will react in several ways. They can overcome it, challenge it, live in it, or fall victim to it . . . For those of us who are decades removed from "the struggle" because of our life through sports or business, we now have to acknowledge that every option listed exists. If not, then we are the ignorant ones.

That leads me to the looters and civilians burning buildings which you referred to as "scumbags." Here's an analogy: If you put 100 people on an island with no food, no water, no hope of a ship coming, then some will overcome it and be resourceful, some will live in it, others will panic and

*others will show horrific character, which is wrong. But not
to understand that all alternatives are possible is wrong as
well.*

*I was also disheartened to see the reaction of burning
buildings and looters by some. However, when you are
in "The Struggle" to not expect that potential reaction is
foolish on our part.*

*The real issue is learning to positively manage your anger
so you can be heard. It's not that they are "scumbags," their
emotions won't allow them to rationally think through their
anger. I applaud that you have done a great job in your anger
management in recent times . . . but not always.*

*Mike Brown wasn't about race relations, nor Trayvon
Martin or even Hurricane Katrina for that matter. It's about
trust. Do I trust you to help me off the island? If so, do you
have my best interests at heart? Do I trust that you will send
a ship or allow me access to build my own ship?*

*And you were right Chuck, let's not discredit that there
are great police officers in all neighborhoods, but let's not
credit that we shouldn't have doubt.*

See you Thursday night!
Kenny Smith

We decided we needed to talk about it on the show. I give Tim
Kiely a lot of credit for trusting us to do it.

"You're gonna get me fired, Kenny," he barked. (TK sounds like
Jackie Gleason, especially when he gets excited, so even in a serious moment like that it was still kinda funny.) "You better let me
live in your guesthouse."

What followed on the show was a substantive discussion on
policing and systemic racism from two different perspectives
within the Black community.

Chuck started by backing off his choice of words, but doubling down on his basic point.

"Maybe I shouldn't have used the term 'scumbags,' " he said. "But it's irrelevant. Still there is no justification for what they did. If I'd have said crooks, thugs, or whatever, still, what they did was one hundred percent wrong."

I tried to get him to think a level past the looters' behavior.

"We have to acknowledge first that there is a disparity between poor people and African American people in the law," I said. "At first it was on purpose, and then civil rights has come, which is only fifty years or so behind—my parents were part of that.

"So you have to understand it's still fresh in the African American household, it's not something that's far away. So it's something that always feels a distrust, that things are still not equal in the judicial system and in the police system."

Charles still didn't acknowledge that the Black community was in a more challenging spot than others.

"White poor people, Hispanics, they're in the same boat, because our economic system is flawed," he said. "But as a Black man . . . you can't compound the situation by getting involved with law enforcement or committing crimes, because then you're part of the judicial system."

We didn't convince each other, but I would like to think we showed viewers how to respectfully and intelligently disagree on the touchiest of issues. Shaq and Ernie, too, who were there to make relevant points during what was essentially a back-and-forth between me and Chuck.

The way we were able to do that drew us even closer on a personal level. At the end of the segment, when we were already way overdue for the commercial break, I said this: "He has his opinion. We all have our opinion. But collectively, we all have to think about the ramifications of why those people are in those positions.

And I thought that's what was missed [in Chuck's comments]. But having his opinion—that's what we're here for."

I knew that in his heart, Chuck wanted to see the big picture of why someone might make the destructive choice to engage in looting. It doesn't help anyone to be called a "scumbag." But he is often prevented from seeing that because others kiss his ass. So in that discussion I didn't want to frame him as wrong or make him feel attacked—I just wanted to help him see what many others do.

He must have sensed my friendly intent. After I finished speaking, Chuck extended an arm and we shook hands. For him, it was a significant gesture, all the more meaningful because he did it for our viewers to see.

Sure, I knew that he respected me and even appreciated that I had the guts to push back on him. But for him to reach out like that on TV at the end of a difficult disagreement—well, this might sound dramatic, but it was kind of like a marriage ceremony.

We were showing the world the deep bond that had long existed between the two of us.

. . .

It's not all social issues and loaded conversations with Chuck. Far from it. We have a lot of fun, too.

He's a very easy guy to prank, because he's sensitive and has so many quirks. For example, he's extremely neat.

Chuck carried Clorox wipes everywhere he went long before COVID. He was the only person I knew who would do that.

Most people would think that if Chuck and I were the odd couple, I would be Felix Unger and he would be Oscar Madison. In reality, it's the exact opposite.

I've never seen a neater locker in my life than his. In fact, I've never seen anything that neat in my life, period. Every suit and shirt are color coordinated. Every hanger is evenly spaced. The shoes are in order, the ties are each folded and wrapped.

He doesn't even know how extreme he is. We'll sit next to each other in the greenroom after the game, and he'll be talking basketball while cleaning up: "Did you see Kyrie the other night, blah blah blah," while wiping down the table.

Everyone in the room will be cracking up, and he won't notice. He doesn't even realize he's doing it.

One day at the studio Chuck left his wallet out on the table and walked out of the greenroom for a few minutes. I noticed that it was stuffed with cash, probably a few thousand dollars.

"I'm gonna take the cash and see if he notices," I said to the eight or so coworkers who filled the room.

As I had my hand in his wallet, I heard him coming down the hall. One thing about Chuck, you always hear him before you see him. I started stuffing the money back in, hoping not to get caught. I was able to get it on the table by the time he returned and thought I'd gotten away with it.

The moment Chuck walked in, his face dropped.

"Who touched my wallet?"

"What are you talking about?" I said.

"My wallet was turned the other way when I left," he said. "And I keep my hundred dollar bills faced this way, and now they're faced that way. So someone was touching my money."

The whole room exploded in laughter.

"What?" he said, before I confessed. "What's so damn funny?"

Another time, Chuck was able to needle Ernie enough to get him to drop one of the only f-bombs I have ever heard from him. Ernie does not curse. But leave it to Chuck to push the right buttons.

Ernie is a stickler for preparation. He spends hours before every show writing color-coded notes with information that he uses on the broadcast.

Early on in his time at Turner, Chuck didn't know how important this was to Ernie. I did, and I probably should have known better than to instigate a joke. But I just couldn't help myself. As we sat at the desk preparing to go on the air, Chuck gestured toward the notes.

"What's all those?" he said.

I told him, and he started to tease Ernie.

"Hey," he said. "Why do you have all that stuff all the time?"

"I bet you want to rip it up," I whispered to Chuck.

I was just joking. I was poking the bear. I figured he would grab the notes, wave them around, and hand them back. Ernie overheard me.

"Charles," he said, in his sternest voice. "Do not do that."

"Oh," I said. "You're gonna let Ernie punk you like that?"

I still didn't think Chuck was actually going to do anything. Then he snatched the notes from Ernie and ripped them to pieces. I have heard Ernie curse maybe three times in my life. This was one of them.

"You *fucking* guys," he said, not seeing the humor at all.

When the show started, he wouldn't even introduce us. He said, "Hi, I'm Ernie Johnson and it's time for Pacers-Lakers."

He wouldn't toss to us or ask us questions. When he paused, we simply had to start talking. This went on for the entire first segment. During the commercial break I said, "Ernie, I didn't know he was going to do it!"

. . .

The mutual trust that we've built on the set through moments both heavy and light allows us to produce shows that are authentic, not manufactured.

Once Chuck and I were doing the NCAA tournament with Greg

Anthony. As we discussed the show's rundown, the producer asked what we were planning to say about a particular topic.

Chuck made his point, and I agreed with it.

"I'll take the other side, just so it's different," Greg said.

That's a common approach in sports TV—more common than you'd think—but Chuck reacted like he'd just heard something crazy. An honest show was all he'd ever known.

"What?" he said. "Kenny, did you hear that? Me and Kenny never do that. If we all think that it's the same thing, just say it. Don't just be making some shit up because you want it to be different. Who does that? Kenny, can you believe that?"

That's what makes both our broadcast and our relationship special. We are honest with each other, even when it would be easier not to be. As a result, we're brothers.

Do we disagree on important, emotional issues? All the time. But I'll tell you this: In the greenroom at TNT, Chuck's seat is next to mine. On game nights, we're glued to those seats, locking in on the action, talking through our analysis, and arguing and confiding about life off the court.

At times, it gets heated. But if anyone tries to plop down in my seat, Chuck will throw them out.

And if anyone even thinks about sitting in Chuck's chair, I'll tell them not to.

He's my brother, and you can't get between us.

CHAPTER SEVEN

A FEW WORDS ABOUT MY MOM AND DAD

On the day that my mom, Annie Mae Smith, passed away in 2017, I was watching our show from a hotel room in Atlanta.

I was too upset to be on the air, so our producer, Tim Kiely, told me to go home.

I sent this text to Ernie, and he read it aloud during the show:

I love my mom because of so many reasons EJ. she first and foremost introduced religion and power of prayer in my life . . . there is absolutely nothing that's happened in my life NOTHING that we didn't pray about . . . growing up i talked to her everyday . . . sometimes short sometimes long. I guess you would say I'm a Mommas boy! Lol . . . her unconditional belief in me always gave me confidence that looking back I shouldn't have had . . . "you want to be class president . . . you can!" wanna

Make A's in school?

You should you have all the tools!

NBA? No problem! Those who know she was at every event, every game, and every moment . . . more importantly on her passing she made me feel alive . . . those talks made me excited and grateful and wanna conquer and move forward . . . I will always keep that and promise to STAY ALIVE and give that to my wonderful wife, children, relatives and

friends in her honor . . . I hope when I'm around you or anyone from

This point on that I make them feel the way she made me
feel everyday! Alive! Thank you mom Annie Mae Smith

Being the Emmy-winning host that he is, Ernie read my text with
all the drama of a Charles Dickens novel. That's when I finally lost
it, sobbing in a hotel about the loss of such a remarkable woman.

I realize that most of the people described in this book are male,
which is a result of spending my life in the world of men's basketball, playing with men, being coached by men, and generally
spending most of my professional life with other guys. And we'll
get into my dad in a little bit, too.

Make no mistake, though: one of the most important people in
my life—perhaps the most important—was a woman.

If you want to know where I get my competitive spirit, my loyalty, and my family-first attitude, look no further than my mom. I
am truly a mama's boy.

She was the type of mother who, when your friends were over at
the house, became their mother as well, offering advice to everyone. Even Charles Barkley called her "Mom" later in life. She was
never Mrs. Smith to anyone.

I spoke to her on the phone every day. We would chat about
everything imaginable, and she had a way of summarizing her
views on any number of topics clearly and succinctly.

On religion: "Kenny, God never said the cup will be full. He said
it will runneth over! Go get your cup, baby!"

On dating: "I love your father like no other. Find someone who
loves you like I love your dad."

And, of course, on sports. There was no end to her sharp opinions about even the great athletes, if they got on her bad side.

When I was in the NBA I would call home.

"Hey, Mom, what you doing?"

"That damn Derek Jeter just struck out."

"Mom, he's the best at his position."

"He ain't the best if he don't do it when I'm watching!"

To those meeting my mom for the first time, she could come off as abrasive. She didn't suffer fools, didn't back down, and looked out for my best interests.

She was not a sheep; she was a lioness. She was never one to allow anyone to disregard her or her family.

The way she looked at it, our family may have had faults, but it was our family and we protected one another, even if we were wrong. She instilled in us not to allow anyone to break that family bond.

It was often said about my mom that she had a unique insight into people and life that enabled her to foresee events happening. In my book, this was true.

The things we talked about usually manifested in my life. That came from prayer and vision. She is the reason that religion has always been an important part of my life, and the reason I would take a few minutes by myself to read the Twenty-Third Psalm before every game, all through my NBA career.

"It has everything that you need, Kenny," she would say of her favorite passage. "So you say it before every game, before every day, and you're going to be fine."

It goes like this:

The Lord is my shepherd; I shall not want.
He maketh me to lie down in green pastures: he leadeth me
    beside the still waters.
He restoreth my soul: he leadeth me in the paths of
    righteousness for his name's sake.
Yea, though I walk through the valley of the shadow of

death, I will fear no evil: for thou art with me; thy rod
and thy staff they comfort me.

Thou preparest a table before me in the presence of mine
enemies: thou anointest my head with oil; my cup
runneth over.

Surely goodness and mercy shall follow me all the days of
my life: and I will dwell in the house of the Lord for ever.

I kept that on a shelf in my locker and pulled it down to read every day, per my mom's instructions.

The first part tells me that I'm not going to need anything because my shepherd takes care of me. He guides me through. I fear no evil and my cup runneth over.

That was a big phrase for my mom, "my cup runneth over," and it's one that I pass along to my kids. We're supposed to have a full cup, one that runs over to the point where it can't even hold the things that we're blessed with. That's what God wants for us.

We should never feel guilty about having a cup that overflows, because that's the plan. It's a misunderstanding to think that God wants us to be poor. He doesn't. Our cup is supposed to run over. We're supposed to have everything.

That Psalm also tells us that we shouldn't fear people and shouldn't feel guilty for wanting more. These are all elements in the daily life of a successful person.

My mom and I spent much time together when I was young, which gave her the chance to impart her beliefs to me. Back then she was a teacher's aide in kindergarten.

I was in her class in the morning, and because she worked there I had to stay for the afternoon session.

We would ride to and from school together on the bus, where my mom would set me up for independence, one small step at a time.

On our rides home she would hand me the coins and say, "Kenny, pay the bus driver for the both of us."

Then, "Kenny, you have to tell me when it's our stop to get off. If you don't, we will stay on the bus."

That paid off when I was seven years old and my mom needed a surgery that put her out of commission for two weeks. That meant there was no one to take me to school. My dad worked the morning shift and my brothers and sisters went to a different school that was within walking distance of our home.

I worked hard to convince my mom that she had prepared me for this moment: I could go to school without her. There was a big debate in the family over this. The decision came down that I was indeed ready. My brother had to put me on the bus and one of our teachers would meet me at the stop.

My job was to pay the fare, remember the right stop, and buzz the bell to alert the driver that my stop had come. The two weeks went off successfully, and from then on I always believed I could make it on my own.

I still pay this lesson forward with my own kids. When I'm driving with my youngest, I'll tell her to direct me home.

"Make a left here, Daddy," she'll say. "Now take a right."

The sense of independence that comes from knowing your surroundings bleeds into other areas.

This wasn't the only way that Mom instilled a deep confidence in me. My earliest memory is of her sitting me on the edge of her bed at six years old and telling me that I was going to be great.

"Kenny," she said, kneeling to meet my eyes, "I see that you will be great at something. I'm not sure what it is—singing, sports, politics—but I even believe you can be the first Black president. You have greatness inside you."

On the day in 2009 when Barack Obama became the first African American president, there was such excitement in the country.

It signified so much more than just an election, because it felt like a validation for our community.

My mom was excited that day, too. But she did end her call with me by saying, "You know that was supposed to be you, the first Black president."

I knew she was going to say that. My mom had long since imparted to me the belief that I could be anything. I know a lot of successful people attribute their success to proving the haters and naysayers wrong. My success comes from the exact opposite. My mom was a positive reinforcer.

"Kenny, you can get straight A's," she would say. "Kenny, you can make every shot. Kenny, it will be better tomorrow."

That helped to create the short-term memory that, as an athlete, you need. You can't remember your last miss and you can't be afraid to fail. Having instilled that confidence, my mom allowed it to grow not by spoiling me, but by giving me tough love.

"No, no, no," she'd say, if I ever forgot my place in the family. "I'm the boss. I made this happen. Whatever golden egg you think this is, I'm the reason it's here."

That was her way of managing the tricky dynamic that happens in a family when someone emerges as a prodigy. The entire power dynamic in the house changes. It goes from "Be home by seven" to "Pick me up at seven."

It's a subtle shift, but a major one. Then a few years later it became financial, changing from "Hey, Mom, I need fifty dollars" to "What do you guys need?" That's even trickier.

When you're still a young adult, this can all be jarring. By the time I was in college, I decided I was never going to ask my parents for money. But my mom still thought it was important to maintain a semblance of parental authority, and she found a way to do it.

When I told her during those years that I was going to buy myself a car, she said she was going to pay for half of it.

"Mom, I don't need your money," I said. "I can do it."

"No, no, no," she insisted. "I'm going to give you half. But here's the rules. No B's, no keys."

If I didn't make B's in college, I couldn't have the keys to the car. (Dean Smith loved my mom because of this; "No B's, no keys, Kenny," he always used to say.)

When I made the NBA, her parenting took on a new form: she was the buffer and protector, a role she played for the rest of my career. Suddenly it seemed like every aunt, uncle, cousin, niece, nephew, and peer could remember something that they had done for me along the way. That's when survivor's guilt comes in.

Your cousin might say, "Hey, I'm gonna start this new business and I'd love for you to be a part of it. It's three thousand dollars for me to start it."

In your mind, you're like, *I don't want to be in business with my cousin, friend, aunt, or uncle.*

And then five minutes later you go, *But I want to buy this watch.*

Well, the watch might cost more than what the cousin is asking for, but you still don't want to be involved in his business. You start to wonder what your obligations are, and where they start and end. That's where my mom came in.

"Talk to my mom about what you want to do," I would say, citing practice, travel, and games as the legitimate reasons why I had to keep my focus elsewhere. "And then she'll let me know."

I called her the infantry. She was the boots on the ground. She knew who deserved help and who was looking for a handout.

"Kenny," she would say, "you can always help, but you can't be a parachute."

Her ability to keep it real with people soon extended beyond the family and made her a mom figure around the entire NBA. In 2005, when I staged a benefit game in Houston for the victims of Hurricane Katrina, she somehow emerged from the event bonded with LeBron James's mom.

I don't know if they sat together or what, but for the rest of Mom's life Ms. James would ask about her.

"Man, she's a special lady," LeBron's mom would say. When my mom died, she reached out to express her sympathy.

Another time, Mom called to tell me that "Jayson is at the house."

"Jayson who?" I said.

"Williams," she said.

It turned out she had run into my former New Jersey Nets teammate Jayson Williams at the store and ended up taking him home and cooking him a meal. I liked Jayson, but it's not like we were super close friends. My mom would just do things like that. She was mom to the entire league.

.   .   .

Growing up, both my parents attended everything I did: school plays, games, you name it. I would always look into the stands to make sure they were there. Many people neglect the power of just being there. Not cheering, not advice. Just being there. My mom and dad always understood the importance.

The comfort level and confidence, the endorphins that would shoot through my body when I ran out of the tunnel and saw my parents—it all made me feel safe, wanted, and respected. It gave me a higher confidence.

The fact that there were people who would support me regardless of the outcome made me put more energy into the process. Structural support is the reason a house stands, you know?

My mom had a look, and I'm not talking about the look when I broke the cookie jar. I'm talking about a look that said, when I came out of the tunnel, *You've got this.*

Our special connection lasted all the way until the end, when she was suffering from dementia. Once, when I came home for a visit, she had been unable to speak for about seven months. She could still smile, and her eyes would light up when her loved ones entered a room, but she couldn't use her vocal cords.

When I walked in, my sisters said, in seeming unison, "Look who's here, Mom! It's Kenny!"

My mom looked at me and said, "Hey, baby! I love you."

Everyone stopped in their tracks. "We always knew you were the favorite!" my sisters said, laughing.

I assumed that we'd witnessed the beginning of her recovery, but it was not to be. Those were Mom's last words to me.

Fortunately, my dad is still with us, living in my guesthouse. He is the dreamer, the one who showed me how to strive and exceed what seemed like your station in life.

When I was young, he mounted a poster on my wall from the School of Visual Arts in New York City. It showed a multicolored zebra and said, "To be good is not enough, when you dream of being great."

This really struck a nerve with me. I always looked at myself as some sort of zebra in my neighborhood. I felt different, in the sense that I would be great at something, not just good.

What made this poster even more meaningful to me was the fact that the zebra in the poster was multicolored. In my mind, that meant I could do it in any environment.

My mom gave me the ability to believe all this, and my dad showed me how it was done.

Like Mom, he grew up in St. George, South Carolina, a small town where everyone knew everyone.

I would spend my summers in South Carolina with my grandma. Every time I was there, coming from New York, I would ask myself, *How did my parents get to NYC from here?*

Well, my dad was and is a dreamer. He can build anything, including a life for his family in New York City. My creative side comes from him.

One day, he decided we needed new shelving—and the shelves he made had lights that would blink to the beat of the stereo's bass line. He had a passion for pictures, so he became a photographer and built a darkroom in our spare bedroom. Cooking? Just give him a cookbook and the food comes out better than the photo.

His primary job was at Con Edison, the company that lights New York City, but he always had side hustles. Game nights, a furniture business, real estate, and photography, just to name a few. He always needed more stimulation from life than his day job could provide.

I will never forget the time he came home with a gift from ConEd for working there twenty years: a mug. Yes, a coffee cup.

"Can you believe this?" he said. "I won't work for them much longer."

Not long after, he opened his own floral shop in Park Slope, Brooklyn, turning yet another hobby into a business. On good days, it seemed like everyone in Brooklyn bought flowers from him. And every winter he would drive down to North Carolina to pick out Christmas trees to bring them back and sell.

That earned him thousands of extra dollars during the holiday season. He'd spread the cash out on the bed, and my siblings and I would jump and swim on the piles of money. I didn't grow up with a lot, but I never felt poor, especially during gift-giving season.

One year, us kids bought him a wallet for Christmas. From that, we learned another valuable lesson.

My brother Vince and I had a ritual of meeting our dad at the subway station after he finished work. The family had a car, but it was much faster for him to take the train from Brooklyn to Queens rather than battle for parking spaces.

He would call the house when he was on his way home. That meant he was approximately thirty-five minutes away from the station in Queens, which was about a mile away from our apartment. Vince and I would start walking toward it.

Pops worked long hours, and we didn't have FaceTime or Instagram to keep up with one another's days. That's why we treasured the walks home together, and the talks we'd have on them.

One particular day my dad was a little less interested in the events he had missed. He was quiet, saying only, "Let's talk when we get home."

When we got there, he gathered the family together.

"I was robbed at gunpoint today," he told us.

He had been walking to the subway when a young kid approached on a bicycle, pointed a gun, and demanded his money. Hearing this, my first reaction was fear, but it quickly turned to anger. When you're young and naïve, your dad is Superman.

"Did you beat him up?" I asked. "He didn't get the wallet we got you for Christmas, did he?"

He looked at me and Vince.

"There are two reasons why I'm here tonight," he said. "I gave him my money and I didn't panic."

He explained that the young kid was shaking while holding the gun. He looked at him and said, "Look, calm down, you're not going to have any trouble with me. There's no one around but you and me. Everything I'm going to give you I can replace. So relax and you can get out of here safely."

He said that he got it to the point where he actually gave the kid all his money but told him he was going to keep one dollar so he could ride the subway home.

"You see," he told us. "The cool hand always wins."

. . .

In our house we were big sports fans. That's probably no surprise. But we weren't just general sports fans—we were New York sports fans. Yankees and Mets, Giants, Jets, and especially Knicks.

These were the days before everyone had cable TV and the ability to watch any game. Radio was the only medium through which you could follow the teams on a nightly basis.

We used to huddle together in the living room and listen to Marv Albert describe the action with the texture of a great novel (he made a deep impression on me, and I credit my own TV storytelling skills to his influence).

My dad's favorite Knick was Clyde Frazier, so Clyde became my favorite, too. We often talked about his demeanor on the court. He played with urgency while displaying a calm exterior. He never seemed to sweat the small stuff.

Dad's influence on my life in sports extended beyond whom I rooted for. He taught me how to conduct myself with character when making major career decisions. As a kid I was playing on a local team at Lost Battalion Hall Rec Center in Queens. The coach was a wonderful man named Mr. Wilmot Benjamin, who was like an uncle to me.

When I was thirteen my dad said, "You know, it's time for you to take your game to another level and you can't do it in Queens. We've got to go to Riverside Church, and you've got to go have a conversation with Mr. Benjamin about that. And that conversation is not for me and you and him, it's for you and him."

He was right on both counts. It was time to test myself on the gold standard AAU team up in Harlem. And I had to be up front with Mr. Benjamin, who had meant so much to me. I was dreading the conversation, but Mr. Benjamin understood, and I felt better for having done it.

The lesson paid off a few years later on a larger stage, when I decided to play at the University of North Carolina. The hardest part about that was telling the University of Virginia. They had recruited me so hard, to the point where Jim Larrañaga—he was an assistant at UVA then and is now the head coach at the University of Miami—knew my family, and I knew his.

"You've got to tell him," my dad said. "You cannot just walk out of people's lives without letting them know."

I was emotional when I called. It was like breaking up with a girl. But, like Mr. Benjamin, Coach Larrañaga understood. To this day, we're good friends.

My father's guidance was so important during those formative years. And my mother's love and belief made me who I am.

I'm very lucky to have the parents that I have.

CHAPTER EIGHT

SHAQUILLE O'NEAL

LARGER THAN LIFE

When I was recently retired and still living in Houston, Shaquille O'Neal spent his summers there with his daughter and her mom, in a house that was about a mile from mine.

My wife at the time was friendly with Shaq's girlfriend, and his daughter went to the same pre-K as our son KJ. Despite those connections, I didn't know Shaq personally, though I would see him on occasion at pickup and drop-off from school.

One afternoon, I showed up at the school and looked around for my son. I didn't see him on the playground, where he usually was.

"Where's KJ?" I asked the woman in charge.

"Oh," she said, "Shaq picked him up."

Time stopped for a moment. I couldn't quite believe what I'd just heard.

"I'm sorry?"

"Yeah, he left with Shaq," she said.

Any parent would understand why I started screaming. Imagine showing up at pickup to learn that your kid had departed with a stranger.

"I don't even know him!" I shouted.

The woman looked at me and said something that, I had to admit, made a certain amount of sense.

"But," she said, "it's Shaq."

Fair point, in a way. Who was going to say no to that seven-foot kid, who also happened to be a larger-than-life cultural icon?

I didn't even have Shaq's phone number, so I had to take a moment, breathe, and figure out what I was going to do.

My wife was able to get the number, and I called him.

"Hello?" he said in that unmistakable baritone.

"Yo, Shaq," I said, still tense. "This is Kenny."

"Yeah," he said, as calm as can be. "I've got KJ."

"What do you mean, you have him?" I said. "That's my kid. Where are you?"

"Oh," he said. "We're at the mall. I'm getting him a haircut."

"What?"

"Well, he wanted to come."

That was the entire story. Shaq showed up at the school, a little kid asked to go to the mall, and he said yes. He literally went and kidnapped my son. Who did this guy think he was, the Pied Piper?

I was pissed, but then it hit me: it wasn't malicious. Shaq was just a big kid. I'd seen him as the Shaq-a-Claus character on TV, handing out presents to kids at Christmas, but I hadn't realized that the dude was really like that. Now I knew.

The guy was different. He was larger than life. He showed a disregard for the normal rules of conduct, because—well, because he's Shaq.

As I would learn up close years later, Shaq is like a one-man stampede. When he walks into a room, it's like the running of the bulls.

There's a danger in that. You can get run over by his personality. But if you learn to jump, move, and get out of the way when necessary, it can be a thrill. And you can have a valuable experience that changes your life.

. . .

My most memorable encounter on the court with Shaq came on the big stage of the 1995 NBA Finals. The Orlando Magic were a formidable team, with veterans like Horace Grant and Brian Shaw mixing with a young core defined by Shaq and Penny Hardaway.

Shaq was like nothing we'd ever seen, a big man with elite dexterity. In the 1980s, big guys would act big, slouching around with that big man walk. Shaq was different. He could run like a deer; he could break-dance. He could do everything that a five-eleven guy could do. I had never before seen a big guy act small the way he could.

His team came into the Finals hot. In the Conference Semifinals, the Magic had beaten Michael Jordan and the Bulls, months after Michael came back from his first retirement and adventure in professional baseball.

We were the defending champs, but we knew that Orlando was more talented. That said, we weren't even close to being intimidated.

Our team was composed of many veterans, guys who had eight, nine years in the league. Watching them drive into the arena in Orlando was like being at a car show. Anytime Penny got new wheels, Nick Anderson had to top him, and Shaq had to get a car better than both of theirs.

It was like *Pimp My Ride,* with every feature you could imagine. We would see goldfish tanks in their cars, look at one another, and say, "Man, we're gonna get them, because they're too caught up in everything."

It was the same thought when we noticed the fashion show they staged while walking from their cars to the locker room. It takes a lot of effort to focus on questions like, *What suit am I wearing today? Did I get a haircut? Is my car sparkling today?*

Those things require energy when you're trying to win an NBA championship. We didn't think they were focused, and we didn't think they were mature. If they had been, they probably would have beaten us. But as it was, we swept them in four games.

It wasn't until a few years later—after the kidnapping incident—that Shaq and I spent more time together. We were still based in Houston when I threw a big New Year's Eve party one year. Shaq had a few hit records out by that point, so I called him up and asked if he wanted to perform for his normal fee, which was $25,000.

As he was about to go onstage that night, he asked me to introduce him. I took the mic and said, "Ladies and gentlemen, Shaquille—"

He grabbed the mic from me and started right in with a different tone than I'd expected.

"OK, everybody!" he shouted. "Say 'Fuck you, Shaq! Fuck you, Shaq!'"

He got the whole crowd going on that.

Fuck you, Shaq! Fuck you, Shaq!

I was like, *Ohhh-kaay.*

Afterward, I asked him why he did that.

"Well," he said, "it's hip-hop. That's what you're supposed to do."

"Yeah," I said. "But everyone loves you."

That wasn't the only time he thought he had to create a fiction to motivate himself. For years, Shaq told a story about David Robinson denying him an autograph when he was a kid, and how that motivated him to beat David and the San Antonio Spurs. Turns out that was complete nonsense. David never did any such thing.

That was part of the maturation of Shaq: realizing that he didn't have to invent personas or conflicts that didn't ring true in order to be himself. I would like to think that our rocky beginning as coworkers at TNT helped him along in this process.

. . .

In the first decade or so that Charles and I were together on the TNT show, Shaq and I remained casual acquaintances. We'd run into each other in Houston, and on occasion I would interview him on the air.

But he was not accessible like my former teammate Hakeem Olajuwon, a big man who was down to earth. Shaq surrounded himself with an entourage. Whether or not that was necessary, it did create an aura of bigness around him.

After he retired and joined our broadcast, that aura did not serve him at all, at least not at first. Don't get me wrong. The show with Shaquille has been good for a long time now, and we're glad to have him. It just took a while to get there.

As I've said before, I helped to make *Inside the NBA* a great basketball show. Charles turned it into a great television show. Well, Shaq has made it iconic, because he himself is a larger-than-life icon. But the road to get him there was bumpy, to say the least.

When TNT hired Shaq in 2011, they did him an initial disservice by promoting his arrival so heavily. To us, it felt like the Golden State Warriors throwing a parade for Kevin Durant after winning seventy-three games without him.

We had won Emmy Awards and had a reputation as the best NBA show around. We had won our championships. Why did we need another star?

It also didn't help that they rolled out the red carpet for him behind the scenes. When I started at the network, the producers had made me come in and review the tapes of my performances, then sit through detailed critiques on how to improve.

Compared to that, it seemed like Shaq had no responsibilities at all. When he arrived, they literally built a hookah lounge outside in the parking lot. At his request, they also brought in DJ equipment for him to play with.

So while Chuck and I were watching games and preparing for shows, Shaq would be out in the parking lot, working on his DJ skills and smoking hookah. This especially bothered Chuck, who was used to being the star of the show.

Before Shaq arrived, the basic dynamic on air was that I would throw lob passes to Charles so he could dunk. Now it was my job, as the point guard of the group, to throw lobs to Shaq, too. It didn't go smoothly for any of us. We'd contain the tension while on the air, then it would all spill out afterward.

Coming off the set at the end of the night, Chuck would corner me.

"Oh, that damn Shaq," he'd say and launch into a fifteen-minute rant.

When he was done I'd walk away and Shaq would find me.

"Oh, that damn Charles," he'd say, and then I'd be stuck for another fifteen minutes.

I tried to stay away from this energy, sneaking off to quiet rooms to sit by myself. But it was impossible to avoid.

Soon they realized that I wouldn't play sides. If Shaq was off base, I'd say, "Yeah, I hear what you're saying, but you're dead wrong." I would do the same to Chuck when it applied.

I did, however, share a certain defensiveness with Chuck. It's not like we were consulted. The news of Shaq's arrival came to us like, "Oh, Shaq is coming, and that's up to someone way upstairs."

After the first few months, our producer, Tim Kiely, took Chuck and me aside and read us the riot act.

"You guys are giving Shaq a hard time," he yelled, proceeding to rip us and cuss us out in his gravelly Jackie Gleason voice.

We pushed back.

"TK, when do we not make fun of someone for being unprepared

My mom, Annie Mae Smith, who first told me, "Kenny, you can be whatever you want to be." She also told me, when offering to pay for half of my first used car in college, "No B's, no keys." Dean Smith always loved that line and repeated it to me often.

Jack Curran, my coach at Archbishop Molloy High School in Queens, New York, who was a mentor about all things basketball and life.

Legendary UNC coach Dean Smith, who recruited me and assigned his star sophomore, Michael Jordan, to show me around campus. Coach Smith was ahead of his time in teaching me how to use one's good fortune and privilege for good.

Playing for UNC with "Mike Jordan," as I knew him in college. His competitiveness and drive were on another level.

Coming into the NBA with Bill Russell (below) as my head coach was a blessing. "Always make them respect you" are words that still resonate today and helped me to fly high throughout my career.

My friend and teammate Michael Jackson (right)—not the singer—who taught me to advocate for people who can't be heard, and to speak up.

Playing in Houston and winning the NBA Championship was a lifelong dream. Hugging it out with my friend Hakeem Olajuwon (left), the most honorable man I know, amplified the moment . . . and the celebration.

At the White House with President Clinton. Standing there with Sam Cassell, Dream, and the rest of my teammates felt like I'd come a long way from my childhood in Queens.

Charles . . . a one-of-a-kind man. My co-analyst, sparring partner on politics and social issues, teammate, and brother.

Our show has blessed me with incredible experiences and brought together some of the most inspiring people around. Here we are carrying on with Kobe and Magic. Kobe always seemed to understand that life is precious and can be short.

Magic taught me many things, especially how to break the mold—in basketball, in business, and in entertainment.

On our set, the line is always anchored by my buddy Shaq. The man is larger than life—not just in stature, but in his sense of humor, his enormous heart, and his legendary generosity.

Going all the way back to those late-night college talks about life and dreams, my bond with Michael endures.

Selfie with Grant Hill and Jerry West, the man who still stands tall in the iconic NBA logo.

Isiah Thomas, "the most misunderstood understood person ever," with a kind soul.

At the premiere of *Hustle* with LeBron James and Adam Sandler. The film was an experience that pushed me comfortably outside my comfort zone.

Family is everything to me, and my kids fill my heart with joy and pride: Kayla, Monique, London, Malloy, and KJ.

Tuesday- @blackish

Wednesday-@STAR

Thursday- @TNT

Friday-@UninoESPN

It was one extraordinary week in the Smith household—four of us appeared on different networks doing what we love.

I still stand tall . . . but my boys stand taller.

Siblings forever! My sisters, Wanda and Gwendolyn, and my brother, Vincent, have always given so much to allow me to live my dreams.

My father, Kenny Smith, Sr. Among other invaluable lessons, he taught me how to conduct myself with character, as well as the important idea that to be good is not enough when you dream of being great.

or not knowing the information? We're watching the games in the greenroom and he's out in the parking lot smoking hookah!"

TK backed down.

"OK," he said. "You're right. Keep killing him."

It took time, but we eventually broke him in. I would tell Shaq that he didn't have to be a big spectacle all the time, riding in on a chariot or tripping over Christmas trees (both of which really happened on that show).

When he would tell stories off the air about playing with Kobe, I would say, "That's good stuff! That's what people want to hear."

"Nah," he'd say. "That's boring."

But over time, he'd get positive feedback for sharing personal anecdotes. Through that, he seemed to recognize that it made for good television.

We became personally closer due to the inevitable connections and shared experiences that occur when you spend so much time with a person. At first, I just didn't have the mileage with Shaq. With Chuck, I not only had the mileage but had also changed the tires and the oil multiple times.

Now, the same goes for Shaq. I've gone through some intense personal issues with him at my side. Kids were born and kids graduated. I was married when he arrived at TNT, and now I'm divorced. These life events gave us a track record together.

In fairness to Shaq, Chuck and I should also have probably realized at first that our greenroom was not the most welcoming place for an outsider. That room was our sanctuary. We would sit in there for hours and go at each other on politics, relationships, books, movies, you name it. We'd talk trash and exploit weaknesses.

You had to have really thick skin to walk in there. You had to know yourself, because if you didn't, you'd be chewed up and spit out. When the guys from NBA TV are sharing the studio space with us, they don't come into that greenroom.

Even Ernie keeps his distance. He flirts with being part of it, poking his head in, but he knows that if he comes all the way in he'll get stuck in a deep conversation.

Then, next thing he knows, he'll look up and be like, "Uh-oh, we need to go on for halftime now." He's too much of a stickler for preparation to allow that to happen often.

At some point, and I don't remember exactly when it was, Shaq joined us in the greenroom. Charles and I had always sat next to each other, and everyone knew not to take either chair.

Now, with Shaq having left his hookah lounge and DJ station long behind, the three of us occupy the same three chairs every night. It's Chuck, then me, then an empty seat, then Shaq.

Man, if those walls could talk. Then again, maybe we wouldn't want them to. Ha.

.   .   .

The spirit of that greenroom—that hard edge and the high standard to which we hold one another—actually turned out to be a fit for Shaq. He understands what it takes to be a star and a champion, and he likes doling out tough love.

One of the most memorable times his approach spilled over into the show and created must-see TV came in 2021, when we had Utah Jazz star Donovan Mitchell on as a guest after he scored 36 points in a game.

While preparing for that show, I had posed a question to the group about whether Donovan was a top-five player in the league. Shaq said that he wasn't yet.

When he got on the air and Donovan put his headset on, Shaq brought that up.

"Brother, this is Shaq," he said. "I said tonight that you are one of my favorite players, but you don't have what it takes to get to the next level. I said it on purpose. I want you to hear it. What do you have to say about that?"

Donovan looked into the camera for a moment, as if trying to process the unexpected direction that the interview had taken.

"Aight," he said.

Then he shrugged and added, "That's it."

"That's it?" Shaq said.

"That's it."

"OK, cool. I wanted you to hear it."

"Shaq," Donovan said, "I've been hearing that since my rookie year. I'm just gonna get better and do what I do."

"Good," Shaq said.

"At the end of the day—" Donovan started.

"Well, that's what I wanted to hear you say," Shaq interrupted. "Love your game, brother. Keep it up."

"Appreciate it," Donovan said, staring into the camera and not appearing to appreciate it at all.

At this point, I jumped in and tried to clear things up, explaining our preshow conversation and saying how it was centered around him having the potential to be in the class of a Charles, Shaq, or LeBron.

Donovan seemed to accept that, but it was too late to avoid the segment from going viral and ruffling feathers. The Jazz went crazy on us, saying that we were badgering their guy. But what Shaq was trying to do was get Donovan to stick up for himself and say, "No, I am one of the top players in the league, and here is why."

He wanted him to say, "Shaq, what the hell are you talking about? I'm already the best two guard in the league."

He was looking for Donovan to react like Kobe Bryant would have. It just wasn't a format in which Donovan felt comfortable doing that.

I DM'd Donovan on social media to explain our intention. He

replied that he didn't have a problem. He later said publicly that he felt that the incident, and the criticism Shaq received for it, had been blown out of proportion.

But not every player can handle the heat. Some guys stop coming on the show. For a while during the pandemic, it felt like every third interview was going sideways.

Kevin Durant came on and gave one-word answers, especially to Chuck. After he took off the headset, we had some fun with it, asking one another questions and responding curtly. I doubt KD appreciated that.

There was another time when Shaq caught some flak for repeatedly criticizing Utah center Rudy Gobert.

It can be hard for young players to understand how Shaq can, in one sentence, talk about how much he loves them—and then turn around and rip them in the next sentence. But on our show we're going for truth and nuance.

Along those lines, one of our proudest moments came when we had Dwight Howard on in 2016. That show began with Charles throwing a fastball right at Dwight.

"I remember the first time we met," he said. "I said, 'He's a really nice guy. He's a hell of a player. But for some reason, people don't like him.' Why do they think that about you?"

That's how we opened the segment. You could see the shock on Dwight's face. I don't know exactly what he expected, but I'm sure it wasn't that.

What followed was great television. Dwight opened up and let his guard down. He forgot he was on TV—which is what we do every night; that's the whole key to the authenticity—and engaged in a real conversation.

Because the interview was going so well, Tim Kiely refused to cut to commercial. ESPN would never do that. Neither would ABC, NBC, or anyone else.

That's the special chemistry we have on our show: me, Chuck, and now Shaq, too.

. . .

As the years went on and Shaq and I got to know each other on deeper and deeper levels, I began to realize that one of his primary influences on me was in improving my business mind.

At first, his extremism with money showed itself in his generous side, however misplaced that might have been. That was in evidence in his kidnapping of a young KJ, and he still acts that way with my daughter London.

Once at the studio, London and I were FaceTiming, and she happened to mention a dollhouse she wanted. Three days later, the biggest dollhouse you could ever imagine showed up at my house. He just went and bought it.

"Shaq, you can't just buy her stuff like that," I said.

Another time, she was talking to me about wanting a dog. Shaq butted into the conversation.

"What kind of dog?" he said.

"Yo, Shaq," I said. "Wait. Don't send a dog to my house. Like, no."

He looked at me like I was the crazy one.

"Why not?" he said. "She's a good kid. Why are you saying no?"

Shaq isn't only large with his spending and generosity, though. He's smart and ambitious about business in ways that have rubbed off on me.

Over the past year or two, I've increased my output of endorsements and ads—and that was straight from him. He has always been so active in that world, and I used to look at him and wonder how he did it.

Then I decided to ask him.

"Shaq," I said, "what is it like to be in all these commercials? Does it feel like you're doing too much?"

"No, Kenny," he said. "What I try to do is create this big element around myself, but I'm not playing anymore. We have a window of probably seven more years to do this, where when we were playing it was like fifteen years or more. So you have to do as much as you can in the shortest amount of time possible."

He was right. None of us is getting any younger. If I have this platform for a limited amount of time, will I take advantage of that brief window to set my family up as completely as possible?

Shaq went on to explain that he also makes it a priority to get a piece of whatever business he is working with. Rather than simply endorsing a product, he is looking to acquire a stake in it.

He also has enough of the right kind of arrogance to stick up for himself, which I'm not always great at. Shaq can be a bully, and he can be an asshole. I was always supercompetitive, but it was internal. Being around Shaq helped to show me that sometimes you need that edge to be successful in the world.

All of the people I write about in this book, whether it's Bill Russell or Dean Smith or Michael Jordan, they all had an edgy side. I was always seen as the nice guy, and on our show I was, in a sense, the "other" guy. Chuck and Shaq were the stars and I was the role-player.

But I was a first-team All-American. I was a college basketball player of the year. I had more MVP votes one year in Houston than Hakeem did. Maybe I needed to be just a tad cockier.

Shaq was unafraid to lean into these parts of himself. He went from practicing with his DJ equipment in our parking lot to having a residency in Vegas as a DJ. He parlayed his athletic career and personality into careers in music, movies, TV, and business.

He has passion and execution, and the confidence/arrogance required. And whenever he pursues a new venture, he doesn't content himself with success—he wants to turn it into a $100 million deal. He's not interested in a $100,000 deal.

It's a productive form of arrogance, and I learned from watching it. Probably now more than at any other point in my life, people will leave interactions with me here and there saying, "Kenny is an asshole."

But that's OK. I'm just advocating for myself. Life is short—and as Shaq shows by the way he lives, you might as well dream big and kick down doors.

.   .   .

I spent so much time talking about the way that my politics and Charles's interact that it would feel incomplete not to discuss the same about Shaq, especially how he responded to my decision to walk off the set in solidarity with Black Lives Matter demonstrators.

The night it happened, I hung around until after the show to apologize to the guys for being so abrupt, and to explain that the gesture was spontaneous.

Shaq was cool about it, not saying much—but not criticizing me later like Charles did either. He pretty much shrugged it off. But I knew that, deep down, he was coming from a very different perspective regarding law enforcement.

His is an authentic position, formed by his own life experience. Shaq's biological father was in prison when Shaq was very young and was not a presence in his son's life after his release. Instead, Shaq was raised by his stepfather, Army sergeant Philip Harrison.

Through his relationship with Phil and the values instilled during his upbringing, Shaq has a reverence for law enforcement types that most inner-city kids do not develop. His dad was on the wrong side of the law, and it didn't work out for him. His stepdad was a law-and-order guy and an important figure in his life.

I'm not saying that my point of view is right or that Shaq's is wrong. I've simply never looked at police officers or drill sergeant types as figures to be revered.

If Shaq's perspective is that the law should be respected, mine is, "Well damn, slavery used to be a law, too, and they enforced that."

To that, Shaq might say, "Yeah, but I know three people whose lives were saved yesterday because of the law."

Shaq feels that the reverence for law and rules brought him the lifestyle that he now has. He feels it gave him the discipline to be a great player and develop a persona that happens to make him extremely attractive to brands.

His upbringing kept him out of trouble. It kept him from being the seven-foot guy in jail. The military upbringing taught him that breaking the law was wrong.

I can't relate to that, but it's legitimate for him. And it's why I get a bit defensive on Shaq's behalf when people approach me, with the intent to be complimentary, and say, "You stood for us and Shaq and Charles didn't."

To that I reply, "You're looking at it through one prism. I understand that you feel great about what I said. But you have to also pay attention to why they said what they did."

It's yet another area in which growing up in New York helped me. You are exposed to every possible perspective. Even when I strongly disagreed with someone, I was forced to consider why they felt the way they did. And that mindset led me to think about and learn a bit from being around Shaq.

His allegiance to law enforcement does bring some funny moments. As you probably know if you follow Shaq's career, he claims to have "G14 classification" because he has sirens on most of his cars.

Mind you, there is no such thing as G14 classification. It was made up as a joke in the Chris Tucker movie *Rush Hour*. But that doesn't matter to Shaq. He has a badge and he has his sirens.

Once, when I was pulling into the parking lot at TNT, I heard the jarring whine of sirens behind me and thought, *Oh no*.

I looked in my rearview and saw that it was Shaq trying to pull me over. I could only shake my head as he laughed and drove right by me.

That's Shaq: larger than life in everything he does.

. . .

A note about Ernie: Ernie Johnson is such an important person in my life and career that he's woven into many of these chapters. He's the ultimate assist man, and *Inside the NBA* wouldn't be what it is without him.

But I want to take a brief moment before moving on from the chapters about my TV teammates and compliment Ernie on an aspect of his life that has nothing to do with the job.

Many people know the story of his son, Michael, whom Ernie and his wonderful wife, Cheryl Ann, adopted as a child from Romania despite knowing that he had a progressive form of muscular dystrophy.

Michael had been abandoned in a park as a baby. When Cheryl Ann saw him in the orphanage, she was told, "Don't take this boy, he's no good."

She called Ernie and told him that the child was more than they could handle, but she couldn't imagine going through life wondering what happened to him.

They knew from day one that it was going to end in a difficult way. Michael needed a wheelchair and ventilator and required constant care.

All through his life, as I worked alongside Ernie, I wondered how he did it. I always thought that I would not have been strong enough to make the choices that he and Cheryl Ann made.

With Michael, they had to shave him, dress him, wash him, and do all the things that he could not do for himself. After a lifelong struggle with his health, Michael died in 2021 at age thirty-three. Ernie was devastated.

But as I reflected on the joy that he drew from parenting, and finally the celebration of life that was Michael's funeral, I realized that I'd had it backward all along.

The boy had made Ernie and Cheryl's life happier and more fulfilling. By adopting him, it seemed from the outside that they were choosing heartache, but that wasn't the case.

They were choosing the heart—not the ache.

They were choosing the time with Michael over the inevitable grief of losing him.

They were choosing the beautiful parts of an experience, not the sad ones.

What a lesson that is for the rest of us.

CHAPTER NINE

KOBE BRYANT

RECOGNITION OF URGENCY

On January 26, 2020, when Kobe Bryant, his thirteen-year-old daughter, Gianna, and seven other people died in that terrible helicopter crash in Calabasas, California, I was on a beach with my dad.

My daughter Kayla Brianna called with the news.

"I think Kobe died," she said.

"No!" I yelled, so loud that people stared.

Looking back, I find it interesting that my reaction was so visceral.

Make no mistake, it was a human tragedy that left much of the country in mourning. But while Kobe and I had enjoyed a few meaningful interactions, we didn't generally travel in the same social circles and never really had the chance to get close.

So why was it hitting me so hard? With time to reflect on it, I realized that what was most personal to me about Kobe's death—or to put it another way, what was most relatable about his life—was the type of parent he became.

Your kids grow up in an instant, and you either seize the moment to help form them as people or watch as the moment passes you by. Kobe knew this. This might seem at first glance like a surprise, considering how Kobe sometimes played the villain when he was in the league.

But to me, those personas came from the same place, adapted to different phases in his life: his ability to recognize the need for urgency and go all in when a situation called for it. That's a championship mentality.

I saw these qualities in a younger, more ambitious Kobe, before he matured and re-channeled his energy into fatherhood.

. . .

It was late in the summer of 2005. Like many other Americans, I was at home, glued to CNN's coverage of Hurricane Katrina, a Category 5 storm that was ripping through the Gulf states and ravaging New Orleans.

Katrina turned out to be one of the most devastating natural disasters in this country's history, killing more than 1,800 people and causing approximately $160 billion in damage.

Among the many other haunting images, the footage of people standing on rooftops for days without food and water hit me especially hard. This was happening in Louisiana, but the people could easily have been from the place where I grew up in LeFrak City, Queens.

These folks, stuck and seemingly forgotten, looked like me, dressed like me, and could have been me. Those scenes will forever be seared into the minds of Black Americans, because the country had failed to help in a crucial time.

Naturally, I wondered what I could do. My first call was to David Levy, then the president of TNT. David and I had a relationship in which we didn't speak as an executive to an employee, but as friends. We would debate sports, social issues, how to shoot pool—you name it.

"Yo, man, I gotta do something," I said. "I can't just sit here watching these people."

We talked through a few ideas, and then it hit me: I could put on a benefit game. David was receptive.

"Yeah, we should do that," he said. "We can do it next summer."

"No," I said. "Let's do it Friday."

This was a Monday. The timing I suggested was admittedly crazy. But I knew that by the next summer people would forget the details of what had happened, and how horrible it had actually been.

"Give me an hour," I said. "I'll call you back."

I first reached out to a contact at the Toyota Center, the arena where I'd won back-to-back championships with the Houston Rockets. They offered to host. All I had to do was pay the workers. It was an incredible act of generosity that I will forever appreciate.

I then called Rob Pelinka, now the general manager of the Los Angeles Lakers but still an agent at the time. Rob told me to hold on for one moment, then he patched in his famous client. At the time, Kobe and I were practically strangers. But my instincts told me that he was the person who would get this idea rolling and help make it a reality.

"Hey, what's up, man?" Kobe said after Rob patched him in.

"Kobe, I've got Kenny Smith on the phone."

I started to explain what I was doing. I didn't know Kobe personally, so I was unsure how he would respond. As I was laying it out for Kobe, he cut me off.

"Yo yo yo yo, Kenny, stop," he said. "I'm in. This is what needs to be done. I'm in. Just tell me what I need to do."

The only element I had in place was the arena. The rest was a blank slate. I brainstormed while pitching the idea to Kobe.

"What I really want to do is rent vans or trucks and have everyone hand out supplies," I said.

"Great," Kobe said. "How much is that?"

"Let's say about fifteen thousand per guy," I said.

"All right," he said. "I'll send it to you as soon as you have it all in order."

Kobe was on board, no questions asked. It was that easy.

Next I called Kevin Garnett. He was a little more sly.

"Yeah, man, good idea," he said, before adding: "Who's playing?"

This must have been why my instinct was to call Kobe first. Kobe was not going to say, "Who's playing?" He was going to say, "I'm gonna go hoop. That's what I do. Because I'm there, they're gonna hoop." That's how champions think.

"Kobe's in," I told KG.

"Oh, Kobe's in?" he said. "OK. I'm in."

Then I called Carmelo Anthony. He was on vacation with his future wife, La La.

"Who's playing?" he said.

"I've got KG and Kobe."

I could hear him yelling out to La La. "That whole hurricane thing, they're doing a benefit game."

"You gotta play!" she said in the background.

It was time to call David Levy back.

"Who you got?" he said.

"Kobe, KG, and Melo so far."

"No, you don't," he said.

"I swear!"

Now he took me seriously.

"Let's call David Stern," he said.

Before long, twenty-six guys had agreed to come to Houston. They paid for themselves to get there and contributed $15,000 each to play in the game. All I did was take care of the hotels. And it was all because Kobe said yes, no questions asked.

The day of the game, we had this collection of NBA stars on a bus, heading to visit shelters where many storm refugees from New Orleans were staying.

Tracy McGrady was there. Allen Iverson. Tyronn Lue. Ron

Artest. Jermaine O'Neal. Vince Carter. Gilbert Arenas. Dwyane Wade. Amar'e Stoudemire. LeBron James, in his second year in the league and on the rise.

I stood at the front of the bus and gave a simple speech.

"We appreciate you guys coming," I said. "Oh, by the way, I know some of you guys have jewelry. Just tuck it in, because some of these people lost everything. Just be mindful. But I really appreciate you guys coming."

I thought that was it, but then Kobe got up.

"Wait one second, Kenny," he said, then turned to address the group. "Listen up, everybody. It's good y'all came, but I'm letting you know that I come to play serious. If you don't play hard, I'm gonna bust your ass."

I looked around the bus. No one said a word. No one even laughed, because they weren't sure if Kobe was joking.

Welp, I thought, sitting down. *I guess we should be ready to play.*

When I thought about it later, I realized that Kobe wanted it to be known, in a bus full of alphas, that he was the true alpha—even in a charity game.

The night that followed was a real scene. Kanye West showed up, still an up-and-coming artist and fresh off causing a national firestorm by saying "George Bush doesn't care about Black people" on a live telethon. His appearance wasn't planned, but he ended up singing a few verses of "Gold Digger" after Stephon Marbury ran over to him and handed him a mic.

Kobe was like, "Man, I want to meet that dude Kanye."

"Yo, Kanye," I said. "Kobe wants to meet you."

It was one of those magical nights. I introduced them, and they later went on to do a commercial together.

That was one of just a few occasions in which I was able to spend extended time with Kobe. Another was in 2006, when he came on the TNT set to hash it out with Charles Barkley over criticism Charles had levied against him.

That year, the Lakers dropped a first round playoff series against the Phoenix Suns. In a 121–90 loss in game seven, Kobe took just three shots and scored one point in the second half.

On the show that night, Charles said that Kobe should have taken over the game. Kobe responded by sending Charles a flurry of angry texts in the middle of the night.

We invited Kobe to the show. After addressing the conflict with Charles, he stayed on the set for the rest of the night. That's not a short assignment—when you come on with us, you're there for six hours. It gave us a lot of downtime to chat.

When it was just me and Kobe, I asked about his relationship with Shaq, which had been analyzed endlessly when the two played together on those great Lakers teams.

"How did you guys really get along?" I said.

He knew I was alluding to the reported tensions between them, which had been rumored to lead to the eventual trade of Shaq to Miami, and he immediately downplayed it.

"Nah, Kenny, we got along fine," he said. "We're just different. I never asked for him to be traded. I never said anything."

"Yeah, Kobe," I said. "But you not saying anything says everything. Because if you would have said, 'I want to play with him,' they're not trading Shaq."

"You're right," he said, and then added a simple, firm sentence: "But I can win without him."

Two years later, we were in the arena broadcasting the Western Conference Finals. The Lakers had recently traded for big man Pau Gasol.

Kobe looked over at me from the floor and screamed, "I got what I need now!"

He knew right then that he could win his first championship without Shaq.

We stayed in the same hotel during that series, and he would walk into the lobby after games yelling, "I smell blood!"

Kobe was in no mood to relinquish his status as top dog in the league that year, as I learned from watching that championship run—and also in a tense interaction about LeBron that I had with Kobe soon after.

Those were the early years of LeBron's superstardom, when he was well on his way to becoming one of the best players of all time. That off-season, he embarked on a five-city tour to promote *More Than a Game,* a documentary about his rise to stardom. LeBron's people asked me to emcee.

After one of these events, I was talking to LeBron backstage.

"Yo, what do you think about our team?" he said.

"Oh," I said, suddenly feeling like my dad giving one of those tough-love speeches. "You ain't gonna want to hear what I have to say."

"What do you mean?" he said, taken aback.

"Well," I said. "You won an MVP. You're an All-Star. You're the best player in the league right now. You even had a movie made about you. And I still think you have holes in your game."

He wanted me to go on, so I did.

"You don't really post up well," I told him.

I added a few basketball points that I'll keep between us, then said, "But you're not gonna believe me because you just got a movie made about your life and you won MVP. It's hard to work hard when you're sleeping in silk robes."

Soon after, I ran into Kobe and casually mentioned this conversation. He looked at me like I was nuts.

"What the fuck did you do that for?" he yelled.

"What?" I said.

"You're not his coach! Why are you trying to get him better?"

The reaction confirmed for me that the feedback I'd given LeBron was accurate. If I hadn't been right, it wouldn't have rattled Kobe like that.

"What the fuck are you telling him that for?" he went on. "Did y'all grow up on the same AAU team together? What the fuck?"

Kobe had put in the work to be the best and wasn't ready to relinquish the crown as king of the league. He didn't want anyone else who was close to his level to get that information.

"OK, my bad, Kobe," I said. "Never again."

Kobe had that killer instinct, but as he got older, he was able to refocus his ability to go all in on parenting and coaching. Not long after the helicopter crash, ESPN anchor Elle Duncan spoke movingly on *SportsCenter* about Kobe's devotion to his four daughters.

"I would have five more girls if I could," Duncan recalled Kobe telling her. "I'm a girl dad."

This, combined with touching images of Kobe sitting courtside at games with Gianna—whom everyone called "Gigi"—instructing her on the finer points of the sport, struck a chord.

The hashtag #GirlDad trended on Twitter, and fathers everywhere, from sports celebrities like Russell Wilson and Alex Rodriguez to countless regular guys, shared photos and stories about their own love for their daughters.

That hit me hard, too. It made me think of going with Kayla Brianna to the recording studio when she was thirteen years old, sitting there from eight p.m. to six a.m., half asleep. I had no clue about music, but I was there to support her. I understood what Kobe was doing.

I also understood what he was taking on by coaching Gigi. He could have just sponsored the team or bought the arena (although he did that, too). But he wanted to give his time and energy.

What a lot of people probably don't realize is that when Kobe was coaching his daughter, he was doing all the grunt work that a non-famous parent would do. It's hectic.

It's *What time are we leaving? Does everyone have their uni-form? Don't be late. Oh, so and so is late—who is gonna call them? Who else is coming? We're running late—let me call the tourney director and see if we can get our game pushed back twenty minutes.*

He's fielding all those calls, even though he's Kobe Bryant. He's getting to know every kid on the team. He's managing their per-sonalities and their parents' expectations. Every time he walks in the gym, he has to say hello to each parent. He has to take pictures. He has to answer crazy questions.

There's no personal assistant doing those things. He was hav-ing all those conversations every day. This was Kobe Bryant, mind you. He had been in the spotlight for most of his life, and now he'd surely prefer to step back into a more private existence. As a coach, he had to do the opposite.

That was a big commitment for a guy who could have been run-ning BodyArmor, could have been running Nike, could have been president of the Lakers. But he chose to be the dad, and that said a lot to me. Kobe was committed.

That is what flashes through my mind when I drive by the site of the tragedy, which is only about fifteen minutes from my house. I know the area well. I used to coach my son's team right there at Kobe's Mamba Sports Academy. We would run sprints up the hill right across from the one where the crash happened.

Every time I see that gym, I think about how Kobe spent his days inside, doing the hard but rewarding work of being a dad. This was a guy who got after it, who competed as intensely as anyone, and who went on to devote himself to parenting with the same energy.

Whether it was in helping me launch a benefit in 2005 or—even

more importantly—raising his daughters, Kobe had the same quality. He knew how to recognize urgency.

Kobe seemed to understand, in the way that all of us should,
that life is precious and short. He squeezed as much from it as he
possibly could.

CHAPTER TEN

MAGIC JOHNSON

BREAKING THE MOLD

I was fifteen years old, staying up until ten p.m. to catch a glimpse of the point guard from Michigan State University whom I'd been reading about. The only problem was, I couldn't get reception on my TV.

This was many years before college games were easily accessible on cable television, let alone on a streaming app.

The legend of Magic Johnson as an emerging player came to me through the grapevine, in newspaper articles and gossip around town. Finally, one night, one of his games was televised in New York.

Standing in my living room, I tweaked the positioning of the rabbit-ears antenna until a fuzzy picture finally came in. Anyone alive during that time knows what I'm talking about.

It was like watching a basketball game in a snowstorm.

Out of the grainy picture, a man emerged, knifing through the defenders and passing the ball as if through the eye of a needle. He moved with an agility that belied his size.

At first, it didn't even occur to me that this was the Earvin Johnson I'd read about. He was so big for a guard. I was accustomed to seeing Walt Frazier at six four or Earl Monroe at six three.

The guy on my TV had to be six nine. He was throwing no-look passes, smiling and high-fiving everyone, and doing it all to an extent that I had never seen. But he was too big to be the star guard.

There was another player on Michigan State, a smaller white guy with a mustache. He looked more like a point guard. I assumed he was this Earvin "Magic" Johnson.

But then the bigger guy, the flashy one with the smiling and the high fives, made a move.

"Magic Johnson!" the announcer exclaimed, then repeated the name over and over. It was mesmerizing, almost like a dream. "Magic Johnson! Magic Johnson!"

That was him after all. The big guy. This was something totally new. Like so many millions of others, I became a fan. My friends and I would imitate his every gesture, from the no-look pass to the Colgate smile that he would flash in postgame interviews.

I could not wait for the day when I could see him in person.

Flash forward to my senior year at the University of North Carolina. Our Tar Heels were in Pauley Pavilion in Los Angeles, playing Reggie Miller's UCLA Bruins. We were ranked number one in the nation, and I was first-team All-American, the best player in college that year. I was feeling good.

Standing on the layup line before the game, I heard a loud roar from the crowd. I turned around to see a commotion, at the middle of which was Magic Johnson entering the arena.

I'm finally seeing him in person, I thought, *and he's here to watch me play!*

Then I noticed that he was walking in with his Lakers teammate Kareem Abdul-Jabbar, a UCLA legend. Talk about deflation. They were here to root against me. Oh well.

The year after that, Magic was my competitor in the NBA. Later he was the reason that I, like so many others, became educated about HIV and AIDS. Finally, he was my partner on TNT, a friend and an inspiration in business.

Over many years, in ways that were deeply personal, Magic

was a major influence on me as a point guard, entrepreneur, and person.

.   .   .

Magic Johnson exemplified what basketball was supposed to be: enthusiasm, effort, teamwork, and smart business.

Early in his career, he signed a contract for the unheard-of length of twenty-five years. He was also the first player to negotiate into his deal usage of the team's arena, which helped him launch a post-playing career as a successful mogul.

Long before his ascent in the world of business, though, Magic established himself as a revolutionary point guard, widely considered the greatest of all time at the position.

But for all his considerable skill, the biggest part of Magic's game was his showmanship. At one point during that first game I watched on TV, he was coming down the court and he got one-on-one, then threw the no-look pass.

He kept doing it throughout the night. At first I thought, *He must see the guy, and he's just trying to make it look good.* Then I looked closer and realized that he really was no-looking.

To do this requires basketball instinct at a high level. As a point guard, you're taking mental pictures all the time as you see things happening. The great ones develop an instinct for where their teammates will be at any given moment.

You can always make the regular pass, but that doesn't bring the competitive advantage of making the defense look foolish. The no-look does that: *Look, Mom, no hands.* It's the ultimate sign of disrespect to the defense: *I don't even have to look to throw the ball, because there is no chance that you'll steal it.*

That kind of confidence and showmanship can be infectious,

inspiring your teammates and demoralizing your opponents. I was a point guard coming up in the years right after Magic emerged as a superstar, but I couldn't personally model my game after his. We didn't have the same natural style.

One way to categorize basketball players is by fine motor skills guys and gross motor skills guys. To explain what that is, imagine if I told you right now to touch the ceiling of the room you're in. How would you do it?

If you stand still and jump off the balls of your feet, you're a gross motor skills person. If you take a running start before jumping, you're a fine motor skills person. It's not like you're taught any of this. It's just your instinct and natural thought process.

I would take the running start. I have fine motor skills. That's also what I prefer to watch. As great as LeBron is, he's a big man with gross motor skills. There is nothing at all wrong with that, but Steph Curry is more of a visual pleasure to me. One guy is choppy and big, one is more agile.

Magic was an unusually big point guard, especially for his time, and was ultimately a gross motor skills player—although I will say that he was the first big-movement person who made me say, *Man, visually that looks good to me.*

My friend Mark Jackson could imitate Magic's style of play, and I couldn't. But I could borrow from the passion that he brought to the court.

Magic might not have actually invented the high five, but it sure seemed like he did. At the very least, he popularized it in basketball. Before he came around, guys would pat each other on the butt to say "good job."

I don't think anyone does that now. I've never seen LeBron pat anyone on the butt. It's always high fives. But before Magic, that wasn't socially acceptable. You were taught to control your emotions and keep them in.

If you can find me a video of a guy high-fiving on the court before Magic Johnson, it will be the first time I've seen it. With Magic, it was like, *Whoa, that dude, he shows his emotions to everybody.* To be able to be passionate about something and unafraid to show it, that was new.

Come to think of it, he was the first player I saw who was smiling all the time on the court. Before him, everyone felt that they had to scowl and act tough. Now here was Magic, grinning, laughing, and high-fiving.

Everything we thought we knew, he flipped on its head: *I'm not supposed to smile? Well, I'm gonna smile. You want a pat on the butt? I'm gonna give you a high-five. I'm six nine? I'm still gonna be a point guard.*

People who break the mold inspire me the most. That's why I love hip-hop music. You take two turntables, which were never used to make music, and start to scratch.

In doing so, you create a sound that no one has ever heard before—that breaks the mold. Those are the people to whom I gravitate.

It was clear while watching Magic on TV that he was one of those people. Later on, an additional aspect of his enthusiasm revealed itself only after I became his opponent: he never stopped talking.

I don't know how to emphasize that enough. Point guards always have to talk a bit, but this man kept his jaws flapping the entire game—every possession, all game long, even from the bench. I had never seen that.

He used to call James Worthy "Clever," because James's moves *were* clever. This was one of those inside details you didn't know until you got into the league. The whole game it was "Clever, get to my left! Clever, you see me? Move over there, Clever."

As the years went on, Magic's influence on me would grow and become more profound. Above all else, it was particularly valuable having a front-row seat to observe his business acumen.

In August 2002, TNT announced that Magic would become a full-time analyst on our TNT show, joining me, Ernie, and Charles. This was a dream come true, not only because I had admired and even mimicked his exuberance on the court for two decades, but also because I knew right away that his personality was going to work with us. Magic's joy was authentic, and it transferred to our set.

I used to say that Magic was the Tupac of commentators, meaning that his enthusiasm could outweigh his rhyme. He really is a fan of the game. It didn't matter that he was one of the greatest players of all time. He would be genuinely awed by what he saw on any given night. He'd watch a great play and exclaim, "Oh my goodness! Oh my!"

Magic brought the energy up in a way that made me and Chuck louder and more expressive than we had been before—but he didn't step on our toes or dominate the show.

He remained the ultimate assist man. When he first arrived, he would say, "This is y'all's show, Kenny. This is yours and Charles's thing. I'm just coming in. Y'all got this."

Just as Magic was always chirping when on the bench, he didn't turn off his exuberance when he happened to have a day off. After a show that he wasn't on, he would call to compliment me on a point I had made.

"That's the greatest basketball comment I've ever heard!" he'd say.

On days when he was on the show, we'd have time to kill prior to going in and preparing for the seven p.m. broadcast. Often, I would get a call from Magic at noon.

"What you doing, K-Smith?" he'd say.

"I'm in the room relaxing," I'd answer. "What you doing?"

"Let's go hoop!"

He would find a gym in the Atlanta area for us to either play in a pickup game or go one-on-one full court with me.

Afterward, we would go out to eat, then get ready for the show. Once we arrived at the set, we would talk basketball all night. For about a year and a half, this was our ritual. Over our lunches, as Magic and I talked basketball, I gradually got to see his other side.

Every so often he would take a call from a business contact, and I couldn't help but listen to his side of the conversation. He was talking to all sorts of brands, corporations, and well-connected people.

This piqued my interest, because I had always thought of myself as a natural entrepreneur. From the time I was seventeen years old, I never asked my parents for money. Money was never a source of stress or worry for me, because I was always coming up with ideas to make it and willing to put in the work to implement those ideas.

In college, I had shoeboxes full of cash in my room from reselling shoes. It was a simple hustle. On trips home to New York, I had access to a wider variety of cool sneakers than was available in North Carolina. It seemed like all my friends at UNC wore size 10 or 11, so I would wear each pair a few times and then sell them.

That alone didn't generate enough income, so I started cutting hair. I'd been cutting my own hair anyway and knew how to do it. Why not charge ten bucks to offer the service to others?

I earned more when I started thinking bigger about the local basketball camps around North Carolina. College players used to be able to pocket a few hundred dollars by spending a week at these camps and working as a counselor/basketball instructor.

There was one at Campbell University in Buies Creek, North Carolina, that paid substantially more than the others, about eight hundred dollars for the week. Because of this, everyone on the team wanted to work at Campbell.

But my mindset was, *They're paying eight hundred dollars per week? That means there is real money in this. How can I get a bigger piece of the pie?*

I dug deeper, calculating that since the school was likely using the court for free and charging eight hundred kids three hundred dollars each for the week, they had money to spare. I approached Angela Lee, a legendary secretary who'd been at UNC for four decades and who became like family to me.

"How much does Coach pay for a guest speaker?" I asked, referring to the alumni like Michael Jordan who sometimes returned at Dean Smith's request to deliver a motivational talk to the current players.

Angela told me that the rate for that was about five hundred dollars, but most of the pros didn't take the money because it was Coach Smith. I was still a college player, but a high-profile one. What if I billed myself as a guest speaker, not a counselor, and charged three hundred dollars for an appearance?

I asked Angela to notify every camp in the area that I was available, but only in that capacity. Soon I was driving to three camps a day and pulling in nine hundred dollars as a speaker. That's forty-five hundred dollars per week, or nearly five times more than what I would have made as a counselor.

I developed my talk as a mash-up of what I'd taken from a few guys who'd been good at it. There was a former Harlem Globetrotter from New York named Bobby Hunter who would come down and show us two-ball drills. He was a great speaker. In high school, I had seen Rick Pitino give a compelling speech.

I incorporated several influences—Hunter's entertainment value with the ball tricks, some words from Pitino and a few others— and combined them with my own thoughts to create a new speech.

Before long, word got around that I had a strong presentation, and I became even more in demand. It got to a point where I couldn't even fulfill all the requests, and I was so busy that I had to make the presentations physical enough so they could double as my off-season workouts.

From all this work, I was able to buy myself a car. Unlike many of my classmates, I never had to ask my parents for that (as I mentioned earlier, my mom insisted on paying for half of it anyway).

All of this is to say that I had an instinct for entrepreneurial behavior. But I had never refined it or learned enough about becoming truly successful in the boardroom.

Magic was on a whole other level. It blew my mind that he had negotiated the ability to use the Forum to stage and promote events. He went big, bringing in the likes of Janet Jackson for concerts.

This guy is no-looking us again, I thought when I heard that. *Who would even think of this?*

I later asked for the same in my contract with the Rockets and ran into resistance. First, the team told me that it was against NBA rules. Next they said, "Why wouldn't you just want more money?"

To me, my request seemed more valuable than cash. It was a way to be taken seriously and form relationships with people in other walks of life. You would be talking to T-shirt and popcorn vendors, promotors, investors, and entertainers. You would be taken seriously as more than just an athlete.

I didn't get this from the Rockets, but I continued to see Magic as a person from whom there was much to learn. After listening to one side of his business conversations for more than a year, I began to realize that when he'd once told me, "Kenny, I'm going to be a billionaire," he was probably onto something.

I called him one day when we were killing time before our show.

"I need to talk to you about something," I said.

"No problem, K-Smith," he said, cheerful as ever.

We met downstairs in the hotel restaurant.

"I want to talk business with you," I said.

He laughed.

"I was wondering when you were going to ask me," he said. "What do you need?"

Prior to this conversation, I had given a lot of thought to this exact moment. I had watched so many people ask Magic for things; at times, he would deliver and at times he just didn't have the bandwidth. My next question had to be perfect, worthy of his attention.

"I don't want anything," I said. "I just want you to explain to me how you did it. How did you become the businessman that you are today?"

He stopped for a moment and looked me straight in the eye.

"Very few people have ever asked me that question," he said. "Here's how I did it."

From there, Magic launched into a monologue conveying the many lessons he had learned about succeeding in business, especially as a celebrity athlete whose name can open doors but does not necessarily give you the benefit of the doubt once you're in the room.

I committed his main points to memory and have been drawing from them ever since.

They were:

— Know your plan prior to a meeting.
— Know your audience and what you are looking for in the relationship.
— Have everything in writing: what the expectations are, what the deliverables are, and what the due dates are.
— Never, ever be late or miss a deliverable, no matter how small you think it is. If a company wants a promotional sign two inches to the left, hire a carpenter to move it over two inches.

— Trust is the key in any business or any relationship, period. Once someone trusts you with a $10,000 sponsorship and you deliver, they will trust you with $50,000, then $100,000, and so on.

— Make sure to overdeliver. If you're able to add things that you know would incentivize your clients then give those for free after the contract is done. The excitement that this person or company derives from you overdelivering creates a positive feeling in the relationship that is worth the cost.

To elaborate on this last point, Magic explained that the first $100 million hedge fund with which he was involved came as a result of a connection he made over a $15,000 sponsorship. He overdelivered on that project and earned the trust to do more.

When you think about Magic's basketball career, the theme was very similar: he overdelivered.

He didn't have to high-five teammates or smile as he played. He was talented enough to do his job without frills and lead Michigan State and the Lakers to victory. Entertainment was the bonus that made teammates adore him and fans love him even more.

My childhood friend Mark Jackson once told me a story about how he was playing pickup at UCLA with one of his teammates. Magic was also in the game. Mark's teammate was hitting shots left and right, like he never had before.

"You never make those shots when you're playing with us," Mark said.

His teammate's answer was priceless: "Man, when Magic Johnson throws you the ball, you gotta make the shot! When he comes over and high-fives and peps me up, it's incredible."

That's the power of overdelivery.

Magic also talked about how, when he assembled a team of

people, it had to be an extension of him—people whose work he can trust.

"After you instruct them on what to do, you never want to have to look back and wonder if they're handling the job," he said.

Magic said that his role was to open doors so he can bring in his teammates to close them.

"I'm kicking in the door," he said. "Then everyone is going to run in behind me. That's my business crew. I've already told them what I want, so they're going to seal the deal.

"When I first went into the boardroom, I'd be super educated about, say, the plastic that goes around the tube of this new phone that we're talking about. And then the CEO would ask me what it was like to have Larry Bird guarding me.

"So I started to give all that information to my team ahead of time. When we went into the room, they would expand on that, and I would answer the basketball questions. At the end of the day, that's what the clients and partners wanted."

I listened to all of this with rapt attention. This was privileged access to the philosophies of a highly successful person.

The greatest assist man in basketball was assisting me now, helping me push past financial stability and toward financial growth.

.   .   .

On November 7, 1991, I was at home eating a sandwich when a teammate called me with the news: Magic had just announced that he was HIV-positive.

This was a major cultural event. Millions of people, and not just basketball fans, remember where they were when they heard the news.

For me, there are two moments that I recall with that kind of clarity: Magic's news and the day in 1986 when the Boston Celtics' top draft pick, Len Bias, died after using cocaine. That one I heard on the radio in Phoenix.

With Magic, the memory is even sharper. My sandwich had sauerkraut on it. I put it down on the counter and started to cry.

At the time, we as a society were so uneducated about HIV and AIDS. We all assumed that it was a death sentence. And now it had happened to one of the greatest players I had ever seen, the sharpest businessman in the sport. A guy who made us laugh, and a person that anyone who wanted to be a winner would try to emulate.

I never played with Magic. At that point, I wouldn't have been able to call him a friend; we had no personal interaction with each other and wouldn't until much later.

But when it hit me that this man was going to die, it hit hard. Part of this was because Magic was such a likable guy, even to those of us who didn't know him. But another reason the news impacted so many people was that it shocked us into more knowledge about the virus itself.

Back then, many of us wrongly assumed that AIDS was a disease that could only be contracted through homosexual sex. That led straight men like me to assume that we weren't vulnerable to it—a dangerous assumption, as it turned out, and one that Magic helped us to get past.

At first, this was scary, because it brought the virus home to us. But Magic, whether he meant to do it or not, immediately challenged our grim assumptions about an HIV/AIDS diagnosis.

After announcing his terrible news live on national television, it only took Magic a few moments to break into his signature high-wattage grin.

"I plan on going on living for a long time," he said.

This didn't compute. It was a death sentence, wasn't it? But in the decades that followed, Magic has obviously proven his prediction correct.

He was the only player I know who could have handled it that well. I would have been running and hiding from it. It would have struck me as nobody else's business.

Think about it: Magic could have said that he had a knee injury or anything other than HIV. But he chose to become a leader in helping the world to understand an epidemic that was still relatively new in our consciousness.

Even our trainers were uneducated about the virus. They told us that we could catch it from saliva, sweat, and even touching. It was a smorgasbord of misinformation.

In the days after Magic's announcement, the league scheduled an HIV/AIDS seminar in New York and invited each team's player rep, a group of which I was a part. They answered all of our questions, which were as specific as what types of condoms we could and couldn't use to protect us from the virus.

That enabled me to return to Houston with facts to counteract the speculation that was everywhere.

Much of it was based on fear, and that did not subside quickly. In 1992, when Magic decided to attempt a comeback with the Lakers, Utah Jazz star Karl Malone spoke out against it.

"Look at this, scabs and cuts all over me," Malone told reporters one night in the visitors' locker room at Madison Square Garden, pointing to his own body.

"I get these every night, every game," he said. "They can't tell you that you're not at risk, and you can't tell me there's one guy in the NBA who hasn't thought about it."

A lot of guys in the league did not like Karl after that, because Magic was so beloved. I didn't agree with Karl, but I tried to have empathy for where he was coming from. It was fear.

Clearly, the information that Karl was getting was not from the same sources that educated me, and the gap in his knowledge led him to fear the unknown.

If team trainers in the early 1990s—the people whose advice and treatment you sought for all other kinds of sickness and injuries—spread misinformation about AIDS, it's easy to see how someone like Karl could believe it.

Personally, I never feared playing with or against Magic. I was rooting for all his comebacks. When people ask me for my most memorable NBA All-Star Game moment, they probably assume that I'll mention my experiences in the dunk contest. But no, my favorite memory is one that I wasn't even there to see.

Despite Magic's retirement for the 1991–92 season, fans voted him to the All-Star team. He decided to play, and while the likes of Karl Malone objected, the overwhelming majority of fans gave him a hero's welcome.

Magic scored 25 points in twenty-nine minutes and was named the game's most valuable player. I didn't even know the guy yet, but I was cheering as I watched on TV at home. I would do the same when he later attempted comebacks as a player and coach, before ultimately settling into his wildly successful baseball career as part owner of the Los Angeles Dodgers.

My rooting interest in Magic—a seed planted that night in my youth when I struggled to get a signal in order to watch him as a college basketball sensation—was about something bigger than a personal relationship.

It was about his impact on the sport I loved, his ability to break the mold and make a new one—his successful life lived as the type of pioneer that I always wanted to be.

CHAPTER ELEVEN

ISIAH THOMAS

THE MOST MISUNDERSTOOD UNDERSTOOD PERSON EVER

It was the spring of 2020, and Isiah Thomas was FaceTiming me.

It wasn't unusual for Zeke—he got that nickname from Bill Laimbeer as a rookie because of the "Z" sound in Isiah—to call. We'd been friends for a long time, after I overcame an initial dislike for him rooted in my loyalty to Michael Jordan.

We could talk basketball for hours. But this time the topic was different: he was calling because something was troubling him.

"Why does your boy have me in this documentary so much?" Zeke said. "If he's the greatest that ever played, then I should just be a blip on his radar, right?"

It didn't shock me to hear from him on this. The night before, the ESPN documentary *The Last Dance,* which chronicled Michael's career, had aired an episode focusing on the troubled relationship between Mike and Isiah.

The feud began with Mike's belief that Zeke had organized veteran players to freeze Mike out of his first NBA All-Star Game, keeping the ball away from him.

It escalated significantly six years later, when the Bulls finally overtook the dominant Detroit Pistons by sweeping them in the 1991 Eastern Conference Finals. In the final seconds of game four, Zeke and the rest of his team walked off the court without congratulating the winners.

That moment received significant coverage in Mike's documentary. His Bulls teammate Horace Grant called the Pistons "straight-up bitches."

Mike said about Zeke, "There's no way you can convince me that he wasn't an asshole."

Those were tough words, and they got Isiah's attention.

I was glad he called. This was my opportunity to really dig deep with him and explain some of the things I had felt from afar.

.	.	.

The main thing to understand about Zeke is that he is the most misunderstood understood person ever. Here's what I mean by that:

The things that Zeke did during his career are well understood. I've always believed that he really did freeze Mike out of the All-Star Game. And we can all clearly see that he left the court after that playoff series without shaking hands.

I also have no doubt that it's true his general reputation in the league, including the way Mike felt about him, resulted in his exclusion from the U.S. Olympic "Dream Team" in 1992, as *The Last Dance* implied.

But what you learn after getting to know Zeke is that his reasons for taking these actions are often misunderstood. He's not an "asshole," as Mike put it. He's a guy who always has his own logic and reasoning behind his actions and who is always trying to do the right thing. His behavior away from the spotlight often proves that.

As a young player, the problem I had with Zeke was that I was a Jordan guy. I played with Mike at the University of North Carolina and revered him as a friend and as a competitor. Simply put, there was no way you could like Isiah if you liked Jordan.

The first time I met him, he challenged those assumptions. It was at Jocks and Jills, the restaurant in Atlanta owned by the legendary sideline reporter Craig Sager. I was playing for the Atlanta Hawks, and we had a game against Detroit the following night. I'd just been traded to Atlanta five games earlier. Zeke came over to my table.

"Hey, young fella," he said. "I like your game. You could have a great, long career. One thing you have to remember about this league is to get your rest and take your vitamins. Don't get caught up in going out in every city, going to the mall, going to meet girls or friends. The key to longevity is having a healthy, strong body."

We shared a laugh. It was a nice gesture. The next day, I had one of my better games as a Hawk. As I was about to walk into the locker room, Zeke approached and high-fived me.

"Congrats," he said. "But Imma get you next time, young fella."

Fast-forward to the next year, after I'd been traded to the Houston Rockets. I was now really finding myself as a player in the league and looking forward to the test of playing against Isiah and the Pistons with my newfound confidence.

As a point guard, he was a measuring stick. After Nate Archibald, Zeke was the best small point guard to ever play. He controlled the game. He could force his will and make you play in the style that he chose. He was the only point guard who could play fast like Steve Nash but could also slow it down and still be effective.

I don't know how great Steph Curry would be if he played slow. Same with Nash. Nate Archibald could play fast or slow, and so could Zeke. They were the only two guards in the history of basketball who were that effective in both styles.

At the morning shootaround, my new backcourt partner Vernon Maxwell and I were walking out of the tunnel as the Pistons started to file in. Isiah looked over at me.

"Young fella," he said, "are you getting your rest and taking your vitamins? 'Cause I'm coming after you today."

We both laughed. Vernon had no idea that Zeke and I had spoken the year before, so he thought Zeke was trying to take my confidence by punking me in front of my teammates.

He was actually doing a good deed. I never forgot the veteran—who was a competitor—pulling me aside and telling me how to be a better pro. No other point guard in the league did that to me.

But at the time, I was torn. How could I take advice from a guy who disrespected Mike and the Bulls by leaving the court without shaking hands? To me, that was more jealousy than competitive spirit. They were jealous that Michael took over the Eastern Conference from them and could not accept it.

I played my part. I just took the advice and kept moving. And I didn't ever try to seek out advice from him again. But I couldn't shake off the feeling that something about Zeke seemed sincere, not what I expected from him. I did keep that in the back of my mind.

For many years I watched him from afar and couldn't help but admire the breadth of his experience. Zeke has held every possible position in basketball. He has been a great player. He has been a head coach. He has been a team president. He has been in ownership and had run a league, the now-defunct Continental Basketball Association.

Then, finally, I began to get to know him better and see that my instincts were correct. He was not a villain. In the mid-2000s, I had a gig calling a limited number of Knicks games for their TV network, filling in for the great Walt "Clyde" Frazier. Zeke was the team president but had not yet taken over as head coach.

Late one night after a Knicks loss, the phone in my hotel room rang. "Kenny, what's up, it's Isiah," he said, as if we talked all the time. "What did you see tonight?"

We stayed on the phone for more than an hour, talking about basketball and life. *How,* I thought during the conversation, *can a guy who everyone hates be such a real one?*

As for the Knicks, I thought that the style of play that Zeke was talking about was one that only he could implement. He said that he didn't want to coach.

"Being in the front office is a good opportunity," I said. "But being on the sidelines is where you need to be, and it's more important."

He rejected the idea, but a year later he was coaching the team. Throughout his time in that job he would call me for opinions. I would do the same with him when I was working on a broadcast.

But our friendship truly solidified after his Knicks days were over and, in 2012, he became a member of Turner's NBA TV. What had previously been phone calls between us were now in-person conversations. We would talk basketball all night—about the Knicks, Pistons, high school, Chicago basketball versus New York City basketball, you name it.

Anybody who knows me knows that I'm a basketball junkie. If you talk basketball with me, it will be an extended conversation. And if someone can teach me aspects of the game that I didn't know—well, then I'll listen all night.

Throughout my son KJ's high school career I would have Isiah talk to him about being a point guard and a leader. I felt that hearing another voice would help him to become a better player, and it was Isiah's that I wanted him to hear.

Zeke helped my son, a nonrecruited athlete, progress to a level where he actually started games at the University of North Carolina, playing with the likes of Coby White, Cole Anthony, and Cameron Johnson and competing with those guys on a daily basis in practice.

But I don't think Zeke's impact on KJ was limited to that. I think he actually made him a better person.

I remember vividly the one conversation that he and Isiah had that sent KJ back to me saying, "Wow, I never looked at life that way. This is going to make me not just a great player but a billionaire one day."

Isiah had told him that to excel at anything in life you can only be good at two things at one time. If you're in school, you're either a good player, good academically, or good socially. You can't be good at all three. You're going to have to choose two at most.

"If I were you," Isiah told KJ, "I would pick academics and basketball. Those are the two that will carry you the furthest."

Here again was the archenemy of the NBA taking the time to give my son advice about basketball and life.

Our friendship ran deep by this point, but in the back of my mind, I still wondered what in the hell had happened with him and Michael.

When he called after *The Last Dance* episode about him, I finally had my chance. Granted, I hadn't talked to Michael for extended periods in years. But when you know someone at nineteen, twenty, twenty-one, you know them for life. You know what they like and dislike, and you know what kind of people they gravitate toward.

Success doesn't change who you are—it just magnifies it. If you're an outgoing person anyway, you're going to be very outgoing when you're successful. If you're a shy person, then you're going to become a recluse. And if you're a competitor, success will magnify that as well.

Michael is still Michael from Wilmington, North Carolina. Isiah is still very much from the streets of Chicago. Those qualities didn't change, but were magnified.

"Isiah," I said, "why did you walk by Michael and the Bulls when they beat you in the playoffs?"

His answer was that doing so was a rite of passage and others did it to them. He pointed out that when the Pistons beat the

Celtics, Boston had tried to get off the court without shaking their hands. Zeke had to grab Kevin McHale's hand and force a reluctant high five.

"When you see the clip, it looks like McHale and I are being good sports," he said. "If you look back at the tape you see what was actually happening. The Celtics were not going to shake the Pistons' hands. That's just not how you did things in the late eighties and nineties."

"Well," I said, "let me tell you about the nineteen-, twenty-, twenty-one-year-old Michael I knew. He's a person who is an elephant. He never forgets.

"He's a person who, when you beat him, he will shake your hand. He will seek that out. Especially if he's the mountain that you're climbing. He learned that from Dean Smith. Coach Smith's philosophy was if a guy beats you, you're supposed to shake his hand."

Michael is like Dean Smith with curse words. I've listened to his interviews over the years and laughed because I recognized so much of what Coach Smith said in our locker room. Mike just repeats it and gets all the credit. I could tell that Zeke was intrigued by this explanation, so I continued.

"The ultimate sign of disrespect for Michael was for you to not shake his hand," I said. "I believe that Michael loves the competition sometimes even more than the winning. So it wasn't about Detroit versus Chicago. It was about you being the top of the mountain he was climbing and not respecting the fact that they beat you.

"Most people can get over that," I continued. "Michael can't."

"Yeah, I understand," Zeke said. "But I'm not convinced."

To hammer the point home, I told the story from my UNC days about when Michael first signed with Nike and returned to school with big boxes of swag to hand out, and I had jokingly told him I didn't want to wear his name on my butt. To this day, when Mike and I see each other it's like college again, all hugs and laughter—but still no Jordan swag boxes ever come to my house. Ever.

I then told Isiah about why Charles Barkley and Michael aren't friends anymore. These were guys who golfed together, went to Vegas together, who were even on *Oprah* together.

But when Michael was part-owner and president of the Washington Wizards, Charles and I were critiquing the team on TNT. Chuck said that Mike had done the worst job in terms of basketball decisions of any owner in the history of the game.

That's very harsh from one friend to another, but Charles is Charles. If he feels that way, he'll say it. I knew right away he had crossed Michael's line.

I offered a counterpoint, saying that if you actually looked at some of the players that Mike had drafted or traded for—with the exception of Kwame Brown, who wouldn't have been bad either if he'd been the fifteenth overall pick instead of the first—they had flourishing careers in the NBA. There was Rip Hamilton, Gilbert Arenas, Jerry Stackhouse, and more.

Sometime later, the Wizards were playing in Atlanta and we were live at the arena. As I was walking across the court, I heard Michael's unmistakable yell.

"Kenny!" he said. "Kenny! Come here."

I walked over to him.

"You tell that motherfucker Charles Barkley I'll never speak to him again," he said. "I heard what he said."

"Mike," I said. "You know Charles . . ."

"Yeah, I know Charles," he said. "That's why I won't speak to him again. Because I know him."

It took another ten years before I could broker any kind of truce, and it was a limited one. I saw Michael in a hotel lobby and called

Charles over. We took a photo, but I don't believe that they've spoken since, and this was more than five years ago.

Telling Isiah these stories, I sensed that I was making headway in helping him understand why Mike had done what he'd done, and why it wasn't personal to Zeke. We were about forty minutes into the conversation. To close the deal, I presented one last analogy.

"You ever have a girl in high school who rejected you and you wanted to show her later how successful you became?" I said.

He knew what I meant and immediately named the girl. "Man," he said, "if I could ride by her house in a limo right now, I would."

At this, I started laughing. "That's who you are for Michael," I said. "You're that girl. You not only told him that you wouldn't go out with him; you said in front of the whole school that you weren't going out with him because you didn't like his haircut, he couldn't dance, and he smelled bad. You rubbed salt in a wound for all the world to see. You disrespected him.

"He probably secretly looked up to you and the Pistons. And when giving him validation would have meant a lot, you walked by him instead. Now the documentary is him driving by your house in the limo!"

If Isiah had just shaken his hand, I continued, there would probably be a Zeke version of Air Jordans.

There was a short pause on the other end of the line.

"I get it," Isiah said.

Finally, he understood and could find a measure of peace about Michael and what he said.

I don't know if it will ever go further than that between them. Could I get them together on TV one day to hash it all out? I think Isiah would do it, but I'd really have to convince Michael. I do think I'm the only person who could bring the two of them together.

It's yet another way that being from New York helps me relate to certain kinds of personalities: the cabdriver who curses you out before you get in the car, then helps carry your bags. The landlord who argues with you all day, then comes in to fix your heat.

For some reason, I get along with that type of person. Heavily motivated, brash and harsh, but with heart. That's why I love Isiah Thomas and I love Michael Jordan. I'm not sure if anyone else in the world can say that.

CHAPTER TWELVE

HAKEEM OLAJUWON

BECOMING HONORABLE

If you're looking for evidence of Hakeem "the Dream" Olajuwon's greatness on the basketball court, you don't have to go far. He was a two-time NBA champion and MVP of the league in 1994. The NCAA Final Four Most Outstanding Player in 1983 and Southwest Conference Player of the Year in 1984. A twelve-time NBA All-Star and six-time All-NBA first team. A two-time Defensive Player of the Year. A two-time NBA rebounding leader. A three-time leader in blocks. His number, 34, is retired by both the University of Houston and the Houston Rockets.

Those are just a few highlights of Hakeem's personal accomplishments in the sport. But that list, while highly impressive, does not hold the ultimate key to his greatness.

His greatness lies in his honor. Hakeem is the most honorable man I know.

Webster's dictionary defines honor as "deserving of respect or high regard." But it doesn't say why a person would deserve those things. The term "respect" is often thrown around casually and claimed by many who have not earned it.

My job at TNT requires that I not only watch current players but also listen to them talk. Many of them talk about "respect" in the context of "don't disrespect me," or "show me some respect."

But I've noticed that greatness never has to ask for respect. Those who possess greatness simply do not allow you to feel a lack of respect for them. The feeling is necessary and warranted.

Some say that to get respect you have to give it. That is true to some degree, but it's not the whole story. Greatness projects in an almost moral or ethical way, prompting those in its presence to raise their own bar of conduct—including giving respect back to the source.

Dream has this quality. But the most interesting part of knowing him is that he did not possess it at first. He did not possess honor or command respect. He didn't even inspire affection.

The privilege of knowing Hakeem was in watching him grow into a person on that side of the equation. I watched him transform before my eyes. He made an inward change that impacted his outward actions and the way others perceived them.

As a teammate, his new attitude became fuel for the greatness of others. As a friend, it manifested in loyalty, honor, and sacrifice. His focus on the court became as intense as anyone's, including Jordan's. During our two-year championship run, he was the best basketball player on the planet, bar none. He was everything that Michael was.

He not only put fear in the person he was guarding; he instilled fear and awareness in every player on the court.

·   ·   ·

When I first started playing with Dream I was coming off a disheartening setback, the lowest point in my basketball career.

Midway through the 1989–90 NBA season, the Sacramento Kings traded me to the Atlanta Hawks. Sacramento had been the team that drafted me, the team with whom I first found success in the league. But Bill Russell, the iconic coach who had handpicked me, was long gone, and the organization wanted to move on.

When the Kings traded me, I was averaging 18 points and 8 assists per game. I had heard great players say that the game slows down for them, and this was starting to happen for me. I was coming into my own.

The trade that sent me to the Hawks was a five-player deal, but as an up-and-coming point guard I assumed I was the major piece. Doc Rivers, who later became coach of the Orlando Magic, Boston Celtics, Los Angeles Clippers, and Philadelphia 76ers, was the Hawks' starting point guard at the time but was injured. They were looking for someone to fill the void during their playoff push.

I was extremely excited. Atlanta had terrific players like Doc, Dominique Wilkins, Spud Webb, and Kevin Willis. Mike Fratello, the coach, had a great reputation. I thought that I was going to make the playoffs for the first time.

It felt like a perfect fit. Doc was terrific but he didn't play like me. Spud did great things but was too small. It seemed like I was exactly what the team needed, and vice versa. But once I arrived, my career took a sudden and drastic turn for the worse.

First of all, the backcourt was overcrowded. The Hawks already had three other point guards, including Spud, and two shooting guards. My role wasn't clear. Why, I wondered almost immediately, did they trade for me if they didn't want to play me?

That wasn't even the worst of it. The team was entirely dysfunctional. We had players who didn't want to be there and players who didn't respect one another. A number of players did not treat Coach Fratello with respect.

I'd been on bad teams in Sacramento, but never one that couldn't function as a unit. It seemed to me that most of the issues stemmed from the fact that the Hawks had simply played together for too long. They were tired of one another.

Players would curse one another out during games, even curse out Coach Fratello. I had never seen anything like it, not at Archbishop Molloy, not at the University of North Carolina, and not in Sacramento.

I arrived with the attitude of "I'm perfect for this team" and encountered a vibe that was more like "I should have been here four years ago, because they don't even care anymore."

It was a mess. When Atlanta traded me to Houston after the season, I was so relieved. The move did bring a significant challenge of its own, or at least the expectation of one: Houston's still relatively young center, Akeem Olajuwon—we'll get to the name later—had a reputation for being difficult. He wasn't yet the player that he would become, and he wasn't yet a great teammate.

I had heard stories about Akeem. While he was an unbelievable talent, his focus on the court came and went, as did his temper. During games he would sometimes slap or punch opponents, getting into fights that survive on YouTube to this day.

This wasn't especially extreme behavior in the NBA of the 1980s and 1990s, when players often tested to see if they could "punk" you, especially if you had a high skill level (that's a far cry from the way the game is run today). But Akeem could turn on his own teammates as well and struggled at times to control his anger.

He had a particular reputation for being tough on point guards. The most difficult aspect of my position is saying no: *No, you can't have the ball right now. No, you can't break the play. No, I don't see you.* Akeem didn't like to be told these things, and several point guards had succumbed to the pressure.

I'd even heard stories about his screaming at point guards during games and telling the coaches to take them out on the spot—which the coaches would do. Still, I hadn't played with a real big man since my days at North Carolina, when I had Brad Daugherty, and I was determined to make it work with Akeem.

My first interaction with Akeem after the off-season trade to the Rockets was at the Fonde Rec Center, a spot in Houston that was famous for hosting some of the best pickup games in the country.

As I walked into the gym for the first time, Akeem approached me and said, "Kenny, you're on my team."

I was excited that a premier player wanted me on his side and was aware that he was making a statement by choosing me over the current and former Rockets point guards who were in the gym that day. It told me that they didn't have his respect or admiration. I vowed that the same would not happen to me.

It seemed like we were off to a good start.

OK, I thought. *This dude is treating me like a real star.*

When the game ended, he walked off the court without saying anything.

"Akeem," I said. "Are you leaving?"

He turned around, appearing a bit shocked that someone would address him directly and without any fear.

"Yes," he said. "Why?"

"Because you didn't give me a high five or anything," I said. "I don't know if you wanted to get lunch or what."

My intent was twofold: I wanted Akeem to realize that I acknowledged and respected him—but I also wanted him to acknowledge me, to say good-bye to me as I would to him. I wanted him to feel seen and to know that I expected the same.

After the game, no other teammates acknowledged Akeem. They all seemed to assume that he didn't want to be bothered, when in fact that was a misunderstanding born of a cultural disconnect that had compounded for years.

.   .   .

Let me pause here to say a few words about my philosophy of what makes a great point guard, a process that I needed in order to meet the challenge of getting through to Akeem.

It's all about understanding your teammates on a deep level—not just who they are on the basketball court, but who they are as humans. What is their background? What is their cultural perspective?

This is what a point guard has to do: read the team. I'm sure Bob Cousy said things to Bill Russell that only he knew Bill needed to hear.

This is yet another area in life where my experience growing up in New York City came in handy. Among the many cultures to which I was exposed, I knew folks from the sizable African community in Queens. Some of my best friends had emigrated from Africa, just as Akeem had. This gave me a head start over most of Akeem's other teammates, past and present.

The Africans I knew in New York had a very direct way of speaking, which could be perceived as rude but was actually a sign of respect. That is just one of many differences I observed between an American Black household and an African Black household.

The African households I knew were very strict. The rules were the rules, and breaking them meant severe consequences. If you were told to be home at 9:00, that meant 8:30, not 9:03.

We look at our parents as mentors, but the African kids I knew treated their parents as the king and queen of the household. I always found that my African friends were more diligent with their schoolwork than my American friends.

Many of them seemed to know what they were going to be in life at a young age. When you expect to be a doctor at eight or nine years old, your study habits will be different. It's no nonsense, no excuses.

Those cultural divides served to disconnect Akeem from his teammates in the early years, and neither he nor they made much of an effort to bridge them. His religious background deepened the gap.

There are significant differences between the Nation of Islam and its leader, Louis Farrakhan, and African Muslims—one of them being, in my estimation, that there is no history of the horrific incidents of slavery perpetrated by the American white man in the teachings of the African religion.

At any rate, most Houstonians in the 1990s didn't understand the differences. Because of my background in the melting pot of New York, I did. I also knew to avoid certain mindsets about "foreignness" that many Americans fall into. As a culture, we can be so caught up in our own sense of superiority that we look at accents as signs of weakness. We've all heard people shout, "Speak English!"

From that very first pickup game with Dream, I was determined not to fall into those traps. It was my job as his point guard to realize that getting to know him would require a different process than getting to know, say, the Alabama-born Robert Horry.

Another of my favorite teammates, Vernon Maxwell, grew up in Florida. I fought to keep his culture alive in the team's dynamic, too. This was my job as the point guard, to make everyone feel as comfortable as possible and create an environment that would bring out their best.

With Dream, the challenges at first were steep. Miscommunications, along with a general lack of maturity, often left him angry. I knew that I had to stand up to that or he would never respect me.

Early on I said, "Akeem, if you ever scream at me like you have to other point guards, I will never throw you the ball."

"Yes, you will," he said.

"No," I said. "I will never throw you the basketball, because the most important thing I have with the other guys is that they respect me. And if you're going to undermine that, I'm not going to pass you the ball."

I said it with a smile on my face, but he knew I was half serious. It was a different experience for him that I brought it up at all.

Soon we were engaging in more detailed conversations about strategy. We would sit next to each other on the plane and talk about how to work together.

"Dream, where do you like the ball?" I said once. "I think I can throw it to you at the elbow and you can use your ball-handling skills."

"What is the elbow?" he said.

I thought he was joking. This is a common phrase among players and refers to the spot on the court where the free throw line and paint meet.

"Dream, you don't know what the elbow is?"

"You know what, Kenny?" he said. "You're the only one who talks to me."

Wow, I thought. There was a lot he didn't know about the language and culture, simply because his teammates never took the time to approach him. That lack of communication often left him feeling angry and misunderstood.

One year we had a rookie, a shooting guard named Dave Jamerson. If a guy made a shot during the shootaround before practice, it was standard to throw the ball back to him so he could shoot again. One day, Jamerson was joking around with Akeem by not giving him the ball back. Dream made a couple shots, and Dave kept it up—so Dream walked over to him and slapped him.

"Do not disrespect me," he said. "Give me my chance when I make my shot!"

Jamerson had no idea he was disrespecting Akeem. He just thought he was messing around with a new teammate.

To Akeem, it was all about honor and respect. At that stage of his life and career, he lacked the self-control to do anything but lash out violently against the perceived insult.

Back then, Dream would also dabble in the Houston nightlife.

Believe me, the Houston nightlife was not exactly brimming with the qualities that make you a champion. Akeem wasn't always on the path to righteousness.

Then, around this time, Dream had a brief encounter with a Muslim man who asked him why he was misspelling his name. He had been born Hakeem Abdul Olajuwon in Nigeria, but found that most Americans struggled to pronounce his first name. To make it easier for everyone, he started spelling it "Akeem."

The man also asked why he didn't ever see Dream at the local mosque. Dream said that there weren't many mosques in Houston, and the man responded that there was one just across the street from where they were standing. He invited Dream to join him there.

All of this got Dream thinking. Soon after, he invited me to his house for dinner on a night when my brother Vince was in town. Dream and I were both close with our brothers, an area of common ground that strengthened our connection.

I remember the evening so vividly. I walked into Dream's home and he immediately began to show me his artwork, furniture, and interior design. It felt like he was letting me into his life in a new way.

He prepared fish for dinner, which he baked in the oven, wrapped in foil. While showing me around and getting ready to serve the meal, he told me that his name wasn't really Akeem.

Then he related the story about the man who questioned him about it, and how it had caused him to begin the process of reconnecting with his roots and religion. He told me that he was planning to publicly announce the change from Akeem to Hakeem.

"Congratulations, man," I said, genuinely thrilled for him and touched that he was telling me privately before revealing it to the world.

Then, to solidify our friendship, Dream went into his bedroom and returned with a small box that was gift wrapped and tied with a bow.

"As a Muslim, I cannot give you a Christmas present," he said. "But as a friend, I got this for you."

I opened the box to find a Versace tie that was similar to one he'd worn months earlier that I had complimented him on. It was a poignant moment, and one that, while it brought us closer together in the short term, would ultimately have a more complicated effect.

He was now committed to diving deeper into his religion, which would involve intensive studying. He intended to learn to read and write in Arabic so he could read the original Koran. I knew that these changes would likely result in us not feeling as connected.

I determined that the best way to be a teammate and friend was to not only give Hakeem his space but also to protect that space for him. If the media or teammates tried to violate it, I would try in a friendly way to keep them at bay.

I also asked our coach, Rudy Tomjanovich, if we could have separate areas in the locker room where Hakeem could get ready for games by praying and the rest of the team could get pumped up by listening to loud music. Why not try to accommodate both?

Rudy agreed, understanding that respecting one another's differences was part of being champions.

.   .   .

Over the next few years, our team moved toward becoming exactly that: champs. The path wasn't perfect or smooth; we had a few down seasons, and Hakeem argued at times with the front office over his contract.

But he was maturing as a person, diving deeper into his faith, and learning how to channel his anger toward becoming a more focused player and more patient teammate.

The difference was never more clear than on the night when he and another great friend of mine, Vernon Maxwell, got into a huge fight in the locker room.

I loved Vernon to death, but he could be a hothead. When he started to lose his temper, I was the guy to whom Rudy would say, "Can you go talk to Vernon for me and calm him down?"

At a certain point it was happening so often that I said, "Rudy, you're going to have to start paying me to be a psychologist." Vernon was like a wildfire when he became upset.

Anyway, we were getting our butts beat in Seattle one night. It was the year before our first championship and we were teetering on the brink of future champions or total bust. It was still at the point where it could go either way. The vibe during this game was not promising.

Not only were we losing badly, but Vernon's temper was ready to explode. Right before halftime, he tore into the referees.

The arena in Seattle had a unique and unfortunate feature: the players and refs left the court via the same tunnel. It was the only place like that, and it was so stupid. Tensions between the two parties could escalate as they walked off.

When the first half ended, we were a few steps ahead of the referees and Vernon was yelling, cussing them out.

Then he did something that he'd sometimes do when angry: he spit on the floor. Sometimes refs would call a technical on him for this, and sometimes they wouldn't. This time he got away with it with the officials, but not with Hakeem.

"Would you stop being so disrespectful?" Dream shouted at Vernon. "Just get in the locker room. Stop spitting!"

When we got to the locker room, I somehow found myself sitting right between Dream and Vernon. While Rudy wrote on his big board and addressed the team, tension between the two guys continued to percolate.

Vernon was looking at me, tapping me.

"Can you believe this shit, Kenny?" he said. "He thinks he can tell me what I can do."

At first, I thought he was talking about the ref. Dream sat there, calmly rubbing his head.

"He's telling me what I can do and can't do," Vernon continued. "When I can spit and when I cannot spit."

Now I realized that he was talking about Dream. Dream realized it, too, and his antennas went up.

Vernon continued: "He thinks he can tell me what to do?"

And then he spat in the locker room on the floor. Oh boy.

Dream stood up.

"Oh," he said. "So you want to fight me? Let's go."

Again, there was a cultural difference between the American Black household and the African household: to Hakeem, if you were disrespecting him, it meant you wanted a physical fight.

Dream grabbed Vernon, and they started tussling.

Rudy was a great person but did not like conflict. He just continued to write on the board as if absolutely nothing was happening.

There was one man in the building who could stop this: Larry Smith. Better known as Mr. Mean. He had been a player on the team two years earlier and was now an assistant coach.

Mr. Mean got between Dream and Vernon. Then, as they were all still tangling, we heard a knock on the door: it was the ball boy telling us we had forty-five seconds until the game resumed.

We sprinted out onto the court, totally discombobulated. When the third quarter began, Rudy—still in the locker room because the hallway was so long—hadn't had time to make it onto the court.

I was wondering what the hell was going to happen next. Then in the first play of the half, Vernon drove down the court, made a move, and passed the ball to Dream. Dream dunked it. They high-fived on the way back down the court.

Dream was still in the process of transforming from young Akeem to the more mature Hakeem, and this seemed like evidence of his progress. He was apparently able to let go of the insult and the feeling of anger that followed and immediately refocus on the job at hand.

Later, on the flight back to Houston, Vernon was settling in next to me when Dream boarded.

"Vernon, come sit with me," he said.

It was a four-hour flight from Seattle to Houston. As Vernon got up and sat next to Dream, I thought, *This should be interesting.*

I knew I would get an update on the way home. Vernon and I lived next door to each other and carpooled back after flights. On those rides, we would have great talks. I was Vernon's therapist during his first years in the league. His kids call me Uncle Kenny. My kids call him Uncle Vernon.

"Hey, man, you guys talked for four hours," I said that night. "What happened?"

Vernon was now fully in his sheepish mode. That often followed his outbursts of temper—he clammed up, embarrassed. This time I was determined to get the details out of him, even if he didn't feel like opening up. He pulled the car over and looked at me with a very serious expression.

"Kenny," he said, "I think I'm gonna become a Muslim."

"He converted you on the flight?" I exclaimed, unable to suppress a smile.

I shouldn't have said it like that, because otherwise I think he would have actually done it. But I was so shocked that he got embarrassed and pulled back.

"No, no, no," Vernon said. "He just told me that warriors like me need to be Muslims to redirect our energy. I was like, 'Wow.'"

I was so shocked. None of this was what I expected to hear. Vernon didn't end up becoming a Muslim, but the incident did help the team.

Prior to the fight, we had meetings all the time to air our issues. We'd already had like five that year. After the incident, we never needed to have another team meeting, because the fight and subsequent discussion had provoked a deeper understanding.

Vernon and Hakeem realized that they had to respect each other's differences. If Hakeem had not been mature enough to talk it out on the plane, I don't think we would have gotten there.

.   .   .

As we arrived at our championship years, two moments, both involving MVP awards, defined the new Hakeem. One came during our second title run, in the 1995 Western Conference Finals. We were playing the San Antonio Spurs.

Before game two, NBA commissioner David Stern presented Spurs center David Robinson with the league MVP trophy for that season.

It was a close race for the award, and you could have made a case for either Hakeem or Robinson. Dream, in the follow-up to his own MVP campaign, averaged 27.8 points per game, a career high. He also averaged 10.8 rebounds, 3.5 assists, 3.4 blocks, and 1.8 steals.

Robinson averaged 27.6 points, 10.8 rebounds, 2.9 assists, 3.2 blocks, and 1.7 steals. Both great seasons.

It wasn't David's fault that he accepted the trophy in front of Hakeem; that was a coincidence. But it bothered me how he did it.

He thanked other stars in the league, but not Dream. And Dream was sitting right there.

"Doesn't that bother you?" I said to Hakeem on the bench. "You just got the award last year."

Dream downplayed it.

"No, no, Kenny," he said. "He deserves it. Don't worry about it."

Then, when the game began, Dream proceeded to dominate Robinson and the Spurs, dropping 41 points, 16 rebounds, and 4 assists to go with 3 steals and 2 blocks. We won the game to take a two-games-to-none series lead.

Late in the game, he came off the court and approached me on the bench.

"Now I'm going to his house to get my trophy!" he said.

"Ha!" I said. "I knew it bothered you!"

Behind this lighthearted exchange was a sense of deeper satisfaction about the connection we had achieved as friends and teammates. I was in tune with Dream enough to know what he was thinking.

I also knew it was the entire team that made him the best player on the planet. Opponents weren't facing him; they were facing us. Together, we were going to take it to Shaq, David Robinson, and everyone else. The league had to go through all of us. It was a great feeling.

An even more meaningful moment that demonstrated both Hakeem's evolution and our team's connectedness came the year before, when he won MVP.

When Stern presented the trophy on the court, Hakeem seemed uncomfortable at first. As teammates, we noticed that and walked out to join him. He immediately relaxed.

In a famous photo of Hakeem receiving the award, he was

actually not the one holding the trophy. We were all gathered around him, and Otis Thorpe was holding it. This would never have happened when I first arrived in Houston, or at any time before Akeem connected with his religion and became Hakeem.

A few years earlier, teammates had been mixed on him. Probably 70 percent liked him and 30 percent did not. You'd hear a lot of, "Akeem is great, but . . ."

No one on our championship team would say that. Not a soul. We knew the transformation this man had undergone, and we didn't merely enjoy playing with Hakeem—we adored it, and we adored him.

CHAPTER THIRTEEN

MAD MAX, BIG SHOT BOB, CLYDE, AND SAM

MORE NOTES ON WHAT MAKES A CHAMPION

Reflecting back on Dream and the Rockets reminds me how many factors have to converge to create a championship mix.

Plenty of teams are loaded with talent but never become champions because they lack hard work, grit, chemistry, timing, or any number of elements.

Even in Houston, we could have enjoyed more years at the top had certain things happened sooner. We've already talked about Dream's long journey toward honor and maturity. Certainly, that had to occur before the team could win. But once it did, we became a team that couldn't be denied.

It's well known that we won our titles when Jordan was in his mid-career "retirement," off playing minor league baseball.

Well, if Michael had been in Chicago during those years (and he was back by the end of the second year, which people tend to forget), we would have been right there with the Bulls anyway, fighting them for championships.

It was a special, if fleeting, time—and one that helped to make me who I am by showing what it took for a group to come together and win.

After years of fighting management and teammates, Dream not only gained newfound maturity through his religion, but also had the backcourt he needed in me and Vernon Maxwell, with a young Sam Cassell backing me up at the point. As I like to say, when I got there he was a Dream; when I left he was a reality.

We had Mario Elie, a fellow New Yorker who had a work ethic and passion for talking basketball that pushed other people to be better.

We had Sam's enthusiasm, and in our second title run we added Clyde Drexler, with his smooth self-awareness and selflessness. And we had the people who fit one another like pieces of a puzzle, none more so than Vernon and me.

He and I complemented each other perfectly. The only pang—the word "regret" would be too strong—that I have is a wish to have played with Vernon for his entire career and vice versa. We could have enjoyed much more time at the pinnacle of the league.

If we had been together earlier we would have been in the conversation as one of the best backcourts of all time. I had superpowers in my first few years in the league that weren't quite the same by the mid-1990s.

But there was a time when Vernon and I had our way with anyone who came into Houston. We were known as the two dudes in the backcourt who were wild as hell and coming up.

Vernon was a great talent, nicknamed "Mad Max" because of his clutch shooting—but the moniker also described his sometimes volatile nature. He played his best basketball with me because he had somebody to pull him in just a little bit. Dennis Rodman had to answer to Isiah Thomas in Detroit and Jordan in Chicago. In a similar way, Vernon had me.

When we went out at night together, we were a contrast in personalities, and we looked out for each other.

I didn't drink at all when I played. When we'd be out with a group, Vernon would take me aside and say, "Here's what you do, Kenny. You take the shot and subtly throw it on the floor. It looks like you're drinking, and everyone can be comfortable and have a good time."

There would be a pool of Patrón on the floor near my feet, and only Vernon would know.

By the same token, I stepped in if he was going too far.

"Vern, you're good," I'd say. "You've had four."

"Nah, Ken, I'm fine."

I would then go to the bartender and say, "Give him half water, half shot from now on."

He was a magnet for hangers-on, people who would try to take advantage of his love for a good time. I saw it as my job to protect him from that crowd. Like, "No, you're not going to just put this round on Vernon's room. He already left."

On other nights, he protected me. He always felt I had too much patience for people. Strangers would cozy up to us, and I'd welcome them in.

There's a lot of hate in the NBA, people who are jealous of your accomplishments or money. Just as much as you have accolades and admirers, you have people who aim to do you harm.

I wasn't naïve about that, because I was from New York. But my street antennas were stronger than my nightclub antennas. At the club I'd be like, *Nah, we're in a place of euphoria, we're good.*

Sometimes it would take Vernon physically grabbing me and saying, "No, we're not good. We need to get out of here."

Our connection became so obvious that our coach, Rudy Tomjanovich, would always say, "Kenny, go talk to him," when Vernon was in one of his moods.

Those moods could be intense. He once ran into the stands to punch a heckler in Portland. For that the league suspended him for ten games and fined him $20,000. He fought teammates in the locker room and opponents on the court. He led the league in technicals.

Part of his behavior was due to bad breaks that he caught in life that I did not. I never had a bad mentor, and he had never been exposed to a good one.

Between Jack Curran in high school, Dean Smith in college, and Bill Russell as a rookie in the NBA, my coaches taught me how to be a man. Vernon hadn't had that.

I employed lessons learned from my mentors to help Vernon through his less mature moments. But Vernon also showed me how to stick up for myself when others didn't necessarily have my best interests in mind.

The coaches I had in my younger years were so caring and self-less that I wasn't always able to recognize that the NBA was a business that could breed a different kind of leader.

I was from the era of "the coach is always right." I needed Vernon to pull me aside sometimes and remind me that in this league, the coach often had to look out for his own livelihood before he could concern himself with what was best for you.

"Kenny, no, don't let him do that to you," he would say.

I was the big brother for him, but he was the big voice for me. My default mentality is to try to be a nice guy, and to trust authority figures. Vernon showed me that sometimes you just have to be an asshole and remember that not everyone is looking out for you.

At one point before we won the championship, we were on a seven-game losing streak. Rudy held a meeting in which he went over film of a loss to Golden State. After about twenty minutes of listening to him focus on the poor play of the guards, it dawned on me that he wasn't really talking about the team—he was focusing on me.

I was still processing the fact that the meeting had turned into a personal critique when Vernon stood.

"Hold on, Rudy," he said. "You're not going to blame all this shit on Kenny. You got to stop right there. You're not going to just have this whole meeting be about what Kenny doesn't do."

Vernon pointed to the video.

"Look here," he said. "Mario, he ain't where he's supposed to be. And look at me. I should be over there. It's not about Kenny."

Vernon was seeing the big picture in a way that I wasn't.

I thought, *Rudy is just doing this to make me better,* because that would have been Mr. Curran's or Coach Smith's intent.

I wasn't thinking, *Rudy's doing this because he's thinking that he has to protect his own job as an NBA coach.*

It took Vernon to wake me up to the possibility that I was being scapegoated.

Oh my god, I thought. *He could be right. If I don't stand up for myself here, I'm going to be the scapegoat. I'll be traded or cut.*

After that I would have run through a brick wall for that dude. And it wasn't the only time that Vernon would endear himself to me by coming to my defense.

On the court he was like a bodyguard. "Yo, I got him, kid," he would say. "You got three fouls. You can't take a foul. I'm gonna take a hard-ass foul on him and he gonna get his ass off you."

"All right," I would say. "Let's go."

It was the same when we were out. When the Rockets traded for me, Sleepy Floyd was the point guard. At first there were some stories in the papers—which were highly exaggerated—about a rivalry between us.

One night Vernon and I were eating at a Bennigan's when some guy started giving me a hard time.

"Hey, Sleepy Floyd!" the guy said, approaching me.

He was obviously drunk and trying to be funny, so I just waved him off. Vernon walked over to him.

"What'd you just call him?" he said.

"It's Sleepy Floyd!" the man said again.

Then Vernon took a swing at him. I was like, *Oh shit.* I was not expecting that.

"He's not Sleepy Floyd!" Vernon said. "You give this man his respect."

"Vernon, what was that?" I said when he returned.

"We can't let anyone disrespect us, Kenny, on any level."

That kind of fierce loyalty earned Vernon the credibility to deliver tough love when needed.

When we played the Los Angeles Clippers in the first round of the 1993 playoffs, their point guard was Mark Jackson. Mark and I had grown up together and have remained close friends.

The teams had split the first four games of the best-of-five series. Mark had a few good games, and so did I. In my mind, I was going at him—but apparently, and unbeknownst to me, my teammates had a different impression.

Before game five, Rudy was going over strategy in the locker room when Vernon stood up again.

"Nah, nah, nah, Rudy," he said. "This ain't it. It's Kenny. Kenny's in here playing Mark like it's his best friend."

Then he turned to me.

"Kenny, if you don't go out there and look like you're ready to fight Mark, we know that you ain't really down for us."

"Whoa, whoa," I said. "What do you mean? I'm playing decent. I'm playing fine."

"You're playing well," Vernon said. "But you ain't playing great."

This didn't feel good to hear, but because it was Vernon I knew to trust it. Now the whole team was chirping at me, murmuring agreement about the apparent kid gloves I was using on Mark. I took it as tough love, because they knew I could be a difference maker if I got my mind right.

"All right!" Dream shouted. "Let's go!"

We ran out of the locker room and onto the court.

Mark had this thing where he shimmied when he scored. It was his signature move. When the game started, I made a basket and got right in Mark's face and did his shimmy. He looked at me strangely.

"Yeah, yeah!" I screamed. "I'm ready!"

Soon after that I got on the floor with Ron Harper, tussling over a loose ball. I was ready to fight.

We won the game, 84–80, to take the series. Walking off the court, I was still shimmying while high-fiving my teammates. To this day, Mark still laughs at me about it. "Oh, they had you gassed up," he'll say.

That was the effect that Vernon had on me. There is a point where you have to choose your team over friendship, and he gave me that push. Not only did it result in a win, but it also united all of us around a greater purpose.

.   .   .

Vernon and I were far from the only people who made that group special. Robert Horry, who would go on to play sixteen seasons and win seven championships, was in his first years in the league then. He was the person who taught me not to give a damn. That might sound strange, but it's an important mindset for a winner to have.

Here's how it came to be for him: in February 1994, the Rockets actually traded Robert to Detroit for Sean Elliott. He was on his way to meet his new team when Elliott failed his physical, and the trade was rescinded. Robert had to come back, knowing that the Rockets had tried to get rid of him.

Flash forward about ten games, and this dude was playing on another level. All the things that I thought were missing from his game before the trade were suddenly there—he was coming up clutch and earning the nickname that would stick with him for the rest of his career, "Big Shot Bob."

One day, I pulled him aside. "Bob, man, what's changed?" I asked. He was playing out of his mind and I wanted to get some of that.

"So," he said, "I don't give a damn."

"What do you mean, you don't give a damn?"

"Well, they were never going to play me here because I didn't shoot the ball enough," he said. "Now I don't give a damn if the ball goes in. I'm taking the shot."

Robert also had a daughter who was born with major health issues, an experience that put basketball in its proper perspective. Between that and letting go of the pressure he felt while taking a shot, he was able to relax. Getting himself to that mental place meant that when the ball didn't go in, he wasn't pissed off. He was disappointed, but he could get over it.

It was like, *If it comes to me, I'm shooting it. And if it doesn't come to me, I'm not shooting it. Either way, I'm just making a play that I'm supposed to make and I don't give a damn what it is. I don't care who gets the accolades, I don't care if I get the criticism or the praise.*

To me, that's the heart of a champion. Rudy used to say, "Never underestimate the heart of a champion, because it's not that they don't care if they lose—it's that they don't care if they win."

Winners celebrate the work, not the winning. Otherwise, you can develop a fear of winning. It can create extra pressure. Champions don't think that way. Jordan won six championships but probably thought he could have won eight. He had a deep-seated expectation of greatness.

Yes, Michael would celebrate his wins, just like we did when we won our titles, but he didn't define himself by them. You can't want it that badly. You have to get to a place where you don't give a damn. The irony is, that's when the shots fall and the wins come.

Sam Cassell was another young clutch player who helped make our team great. He was boisterous, loud, and supportive. Even though he was several years younger than I was, I learned an important lesson from him—to never forget the love of the game and the fun you can have playing it.

Sam was a basketball head like the rest of us. He would be in the back of the bus with the group dissecting the game—but the difference with Sam was that he would point out every moment that was fun.

"We lost, but remember when we made that guy fall?" he'd say, laughing.

What I admired most about Sam was his unbridled love for others. If you made a shot, he was the first guy to jump into your arms.

In the first game of the 1995 NBA Finals, I broke a record at the time by making seven 3-pointers. On the last one, Sam ran off the bench to chest-bump me. Remember, he was my backup. The fact that I was torching Orlando meant that he wasn't playing. That wasn't even a thought on his mind.

I didn't realize it until years later, but I helped him to become that way. Sam and I ran into each other in 2006, when he was a veteran on the Los Angeles Clippers and I was almost a decade into my career at TNT.

"Kenny," he said, "I had to give Shaun Livingston the speech."

Shaun was a young player at the time who, before he hurt his knee, was talked about as the next Grant Hill or Penny Hardaway. I didn't know what he meant.

"What speech are you talking about?"

"The speech you gave me," he said.

"Sam," I said, still not getting it, "what speech could I have given you?"

Then he reminded me. "You pulled me aside once and said, 'Look, Sam, don't ever think that when you're in the game doing well, I'm wishing you're not doing well so I can get in. If you're killing, I'm rooting for you.' "

I didn't remember saying that to him, but I recalled the period of time to which he was referring.

Early in Sam's career, his talent was obvious, but he was backing me up. The media was starting to push the envelope with stories about the dynamic, and I could see in practice that the thoughts were starting to seep into him. I felt like I had to reassure him that it was about the team, not him or me.

Now he was paying it forward to Livingston. That was a good feeling.

"You gave me the speech and it just made me relax," he said. "And so I just started playing better because I knew that you weren't on a bench hoping I didn't play well. That was a speech that changed my career. Now I gave it to the young fella."

. . .

If Robert and Sam were the kids in our championship mix, Clyde Drexler was the wise old man. Clyde had been in the league since 1983 and had made eight All-Star teams as a member of the Portland Trail Blazers. He had once finished second to Jordan in MVP voting and reached the NBA Finals before losing to the Bulls.

After we won our first championship in 1994, we came out of the gate hot the next season, winning our first nine games. But then we stumbled for months, struggling to find consistency, let alone dominance.

In February, the team traded Otis Thorpe, a beloved teammate, to Portland for Clyde.

We hated Clyde from day one. We all loved Otis, and the new guy had to win us over. And Clyde's first impression didn't help. He came off like an Ivy Leaguer, as if he thought he was better than us.

I'll never forget what happened the first time he walked into the arena. He and Tracy Murray, who was also part of the trade, entered and the crowd erupted.

I'd forgotten that he had once starred for the University of Houston, so I couldn't fathom what was going on. We had just won a championship and they were going crazy over this guy?

We all looked at one another—me, Sam, my good friend Chucky Brown—like, *What? They're giving this dude a standing ovation in* our *game?*

For a while after that, there were a lot of whispers about what was going on. And I'm not gonna lie, I was part of it.

It's just that we were seeing things we didn't appreciate. Like when we came back into the locker room for our pregame workouts that day and Clyde was sitting there, reading the paper and drinking coffee with his legs crossed.

Really? we thought. *You're that comfortable already where you don't even feel the need to go out and warm up with your new teammates?*

It was rubbing people the wrong way. It troubled me enough that after a few games my curiosity took over and I decided that I had to figure the guy out.

"You don't need to go out and warm up?" I asked him.

"Nah, Kenny, I don't."

I asked him why. "Remember when I was in the dunk contest?" he said.

"Yeah."

"Well, in the dunk contest, you do a dunk and then you sit," he said. "And I started jumping higher. So I felt like I might be wasting my energy by warming up. Now I'll do a light stretch right before the game and be ready to play."

It was a lesson in giving someone the benefit of the doubt, rather than prejudging. Now it made sense. Clyde wasn't being elitist; he was doing something that helped him to perform better for us. This is why you take the time to figure out why people do things, rather than relying on the image in your mind of the way it should be.

The way Clyde conducted himself on the court also bothered us at first. He was very domineering, yelling, "No, no, no!" at guys and telling them, "When I'm open give me the ball here, like this."

We were like, *No, bro. We know you've been an All-Star and all that, but our team won a championship. Your team lost.*

But just as we learned that his pregame routine had a purpose, we came to understand that his aggressive behavior during games was a result of his hunger. He hadn't reached the mountaintop, and we had. When we embraced him for that, we exploded. It took about fifteen or twenty games to fully accept him, and for a while we were just smoldering around mediocrity.

In the end, Clyde revealed himself to be extremely unselfish. Some guys want an assist because they want to get the assist. Clyde wanted the assist to make you look better. Clyde would give you the ball when you cut to the basket, so you could dunk it.

He wouldn't get the accolades for that. You started to realize that he wanted what was best for others. And when you embrace that—when you truly, fully want the best for the other players—you have a championship team. That is a very hard place to get to.

We went into the playoffs as the sixth seed that year and became the first sixth seed in history to win the championship. We never had home court. Every city, every series, we would start it on the road. That was unprecedented.

We ran the table anyway. We took the Utah Jazz to the full five games in the first round. We beat Phoenix in seven in the Conference Semifinals and the Spurs in six to reach the NBA Finals. By then we were so confident that we took care of Orlando in a four-game sweep to become back-to-back champions.

We had a mental toughness that came from believing in one another. In order to be champions, you have to believe in things that you don't see. I have to believe that my teammate is going to be there to help me when I'm on defense and I can't see behind me.

I have to believe he will be in the right spot when I'm passing him the ball, even though I can't see him. It's like a faith in God. It can be that deep.

And for a few special years in Houston, we had it.

CHAPTER FOURTEEN

YOU KIDS

I started this book by speaking directly to my children: Kayla Brianna, KJ, Monique, London, and Malloy.

In the chapters that followed, my aim was to convey the lessons drawn from the most influential people in my life. These mentors combined to make me the man and parent that I am today. But this project would be incomplete without circling back to describe the profound impact that my kids themselves have had on my life.

Yes, it's a parent's job to be a mentor and guide, but there's so much to learn from our children, too. They make us better and quickly grow into people who have their own lessons to impart, if we're paying attention.

The responsibility of having a partner and, eventually, a family doesn't always occur to a young man. Sometimes we have to be nudged into getting our act together at the beginning of adulthood.

During my sophomore year at the University of North Carolina, my girlfriend Dawn—who later became my wife and mother to KJ and Kayla—nearly broke up with me.

One day we were sitting around my room and my transcript was on the desk. She picked it up and looked at it, which was fine with me; I wasn't the type to hide anything from her.

She spent a few minutes looking it over, not saying a word. My grades weren't great, but I overall felt good about myself. I was a popular athlete on campus, and even though I was injured for part of my freshman season, the future seemed bright. That's why it surprised me when Dawn, looking the paper up and down, turned serious.

"Hey, I need to have a conversation with you," she said.

"What?" I said, still not realizing the sudden gravity of the situation.

"I'm not sure if I can continue dating you," she said.

"Why? What are you talking about?"

"Well," she said, "you're making it with C pluses and B minuses. What are you going to do in life with C pluses and B minuses?"

"I'm going to be a pro basketball player," I said. "I'm on that path."

She continued to push. "But what if you break your leg? Then I'm going to be dating some C-plus guy? Some B-minus guy?"

On the defensive now, I insisted that wouldn't happen. It was clear that I had work to do to prove that pursuing a livelihood in this field would be a good idea.

"That doesn't even exist, career-ending injuries in basketball," I claimed weakly. "Like, you get hurt, you come back."

She hesitated. "I really don't know . . . ," she said.

Then I had an idea.

"Let's go to the library," I said. "Let me show you what kind of salary an NBA player can earn. It really can be a career."

This was long before Google. Nowadays, I could simply pull up "LeBron James's salary" on my phone to convince her that basketball could be a lucrative career path. Back then, you had to go to the actual library and search through news stories.

Plus, this was before Michael Jordan's superstardom, before the NBA achieved a higher and higher profile in the 1980s and 1990s. In 1980, CBS had shown the NBA Finals on a tape delay.

I did the research and showed her salaries in the NBA. She saw that stars were making high six figures.

"They get this much just to play basketball?" Dawn said.

"If you do well," I said, reminding her that it took a working man like my father decades to earn as much as a basketball player could make in a single year. Basketball was not just a game or a job, I told her, but a career.

She thought about it for a moment.

"You still can break your leg," she finally said. "And that would mean you wouldn't be able to practice enough to get to that level."

She had a point there. The conversation helped to mature me on two levels. One, I worked hard to become a B student or better, not a B and C student.

Also, the act of having to justify and explain my dreams made them more concrete and underscored the gravity of my situation. It helped me to realize that basketball was indeed a career, and one that required hard work.

I will admit that an athlete tends to mature more slowly than a person in the so-called real world. An athlete's life is not realistic. People pamper you and take care of so many things for you, ensuring that you don't learn how to do those things until later in life.

When Dawn and I had our first child, Kayla Brianna, I was twenty-eight—but in life terms, I was probably twenty-one or twenty-two. I had a lot of learning and a lot of maturing to do. Fortunately, the best teachers of my life were on the way.

My parenting journey began with Kayla waiting on me to arrive—not the other way around, as it usually happens.

This was the pager era, before cell phones. I didn't even have a pager but finally broke down and got one when Dawn was pregnant. I was on the road all the time and needed some way to find out if she was going into labor.

We were in the playoffs, facing the Utah Jazz. After a game in Utah, we boarded the plane to head back to Houston.

Sitting on the runway next to my friend Vernon Maxwell, I was fiddling with the pager when it started to go off.

"See," I said to Vernon. "This is why I didn't want a pager. I don't even know how to work this thing."

"What do you mean?" he said.

I pointed to the little screen, which was displaying a whole bunch of what seemed like random numbers. "Look," I said. "Someone is sending me these numbers, and I have no idea what it means."

Vernon looked at the pager and then up at me. "Hey, fool, that's your number with nine-one-one at the end," he said.

Oops. Apparently the baby was coming.

When we landed, I rushed to the hospital and searched for Dawn's room. She had somehow managed to drive herself while in labor, although she spared me from knowing about that until after the fact.

I found the room and the doctor said, "Oh hey, Mr. Smith. I'm glad you made it."

Breathless, I told him that I was just going to run out for a moment to get a camcorder. "If you walk out of this room," the doctor said, "you're going to miss it."

I hadn't realized how close I'd cut it. Within five minutes, Kayla arrived. She had waited on me, and that was where our connection started.

As the years went on, she mentored me as much as I mentored her. Being my first child, she was teaching me how to handle this massive responsibility. All the new moments, all the unexpected challenges that emerged—she and I learned how to navigate them together.

From a young age, Kayla displayed enormous talent as a performer. When she was nine years old, we took her to New York to audition for *The Lion King* on Broadway and two other shows. We arrived at the first audition and they handed her a script. I offered to run lines with her while we waited.

"No, no, no," Kayla said, respectful but firm. "Dad, you just sit here. Mom, you sit over here. I'm going to go over here in the back and focus on this."

At nine years old she said that to us. Then she went off by herself and locked it in, as I watched out of the corner of my eye. She was pacing and talking to herself.

I started laughing because I used to do the same thing when I played. I was always like, "Nah, you don't need to rebound for me. Just let me go over here and lock in, and I'm good." But I didn't learn to do that until I was eighteen or nineteen years old and in college. And here's this little girl doing it instinctively.

We went to the next audition, and she did the routine again. She repeated it again at the third place. It worked. As we would leave an audition, we'd get a call from the previous one saying that she had gotten the part. This happened for all three of them.

Logistically, she could only accept two of the roles. One was a no-brainer, the part of Nala in *The Lion King*. That one started later in the year, so we were able to choose it and another show that started right away.

Immediately upon accepting, she had to get to rehearsals in Charlotte, North Carolina, because the production was already under way. They had cast another actress, but it wasn't working out. Kayla was to replace her.

They sent us the contract and keys to an apartment in Charlotte. Dawn and I decided that she would go with Kayla and I would stay home in Houston with KJ.

Three days after they moved into the apartment, Kayla's agent called with horrible news. It turned out that the other girl's contract called for her to receive full pay if she was fired. Since the producers didn't want to pay two actresses for the same part, the original actress was back in, and Kayla was out.

We were stunned, but at least she had *The Lion King* to look forward to. It was the biggest play on Broadway, and her run was scheduled to start in six months.

Three months later, Kayla grew three inches. She was now taller than Simba, and that wasn't going to work. She lost that part, too.

She was devastated. At nine years old, she had gone from being on top of the world to losing two big parts, both through no fault of her own. It was a harsh lesson in the realities of how bad luck can bite you.

I had to gather myself and think, *OK, what's my parenting moment here?*

Her mom assumed the role of nurturing and caressing, and I decided to take on the mental side. That was the type of care I was accustomed to receiving. Your coaches don't caress you, but the good ones help you attain perspective on setbacks and challenges.

The message that I landed on was to question the meaning of winning. I asked Kayla what defined "winning" in this situation. Was it getting the part, or would she only win if she was able to perform in the show? Could it be the former?

If Kayla did the show, it would last for less than a year. She would have been on Broadway, but then it would be over. But even without that, she knew she was good enough. She'd gotten the role.

I repeated this when she needed reassurance and just kept telling her that I could not believe how great she was, how she was doing things that I couldn't imagine doing. I thought it was important to emphasize that over the disappointment.

When you have to dig deep inside yourself to deliver a message to your child in a moment of crisis, it's a real gut check. You learn where you stand on an issue, and that you're capable of helping.

I also made it clear that her preparation had taught and inspired me. I was still in my first years as a broadcaster and not nearly as confident a performer as I was an athlete. By getting into the zone and doing what it took to be great, Kayla showed me that the same techniques that worked for me on the court could work in front of the camera.

That was mentorship from her to me. And when she got over disappointment relatively quickly and was able to move on, that was another lesson for me in the importance of having a short memory in show business.

KJ arrived next, and he was a force of nature in an entirely different way. If Kayla was almost eerily like me with her quiet intensity as she prepared for big moments, KJ was a contrast, outgoing and magnetic.

The first parenting dilemma about KJ came early: as my first son, should I name him Kenny Smith? If I did, would that allow him to have his own identity, his own beliefs, his own life? Dawn didn't think it would be a problem, and that gave the idea a bit of validation. Then Kayla, at just four years old, offered a wise insight.

"His name is exactly like yours, right?" she said. "Kenny Smith?"

"Yeah," I said.

"He needs a nickname," she said.

"Why?"

"Because we shouldn't be calling him the same thing as you," she said. "He's going to think he's you."

I laughed, because it was so simple yet so profound. Kayla was right. And that's how he became KJ. If anyone says, "Hey, Kenny," he doesn't even turn around. He doesn't recognize that as his name. He only turns around for "KJ," and he has Kayla to thank for that identity.

Having his own name turned out to be a good introduction to one of the most important notions that I tried to instill in him: don't cheat the grind. It was obvious early on that he had an interest in sports and the ability to pursue them at a high level. But it was important for him to realize that he and I were two different athletes, and what made me good wouldn't necessarily be what made him good.

My analogy to him was, if Grandpa were a brain surgeon, that wouldn't automatically make me a brain surgeon. I would have to go to school for it. I would have to study. My career in the NBA wasn't going to make KJ a basketball player.

First, he would have to do certain things as a high school player and then as a college player. You can't cheat the grind.

KJ did end up playing at a high level, following in my footsteps as a point guard at the University of North Carolina. But his gifts in another area exceeded mine and propelled him to a different station in life.

KJ is a bigger thinker than I ever was. He's on a whole different grind, and the sky's the limit on his vision and potential. One day a few years ago, he and I were talking about NBA players, and instead of saying that he expected to be one of them, he said, "I can own the Lakers."

I was like, "What?"

"Yeah," he said. "I'm going to own the Lakers."

I don't know if this was more than a passing thought for KJ. But I certainly remember it, because it was the moment when I realized the scope of his thinking.

KJ couples his broad vision with a gravitational social pull that I lack. If people like me, it's because I'm basically a nice guy, but I'm not overly outgoing. KJ has the empathy and interest to form a bond with anyone.

Once when he was a kid, maybe eight years old, I left him in a barbershop for a few minutes to get water and snacks at a store nearby.

When I returned, he knew the name of every kid in the place, and every barber.

There was one kid who had an Xbox or Nintendo in his bag, and they pulled it out and started playing. If KJ hadn't been so warm and outgoing, he never would have had that experience.

Later, he told me personal details about the barber's life that I didn't know. I mean, the guy was our barber. We weren't having deep conversations. But KJ approaches people in a way that draws them out.

It has to do with his instinct for inclusiveness. When he talks to people, he's not trying to get something out of them. He's genuinely curious about their lives, and that ends up working to his advantage.

That's not me. I'm the person who will sit back, wait, and do surveillance on a social situation. Then I'm going to pick one or two people with whom to engage. KJ will understand the whole environment in a shorter time and know how to engage with it.

His vision extends beyond social interaction. He was the one, for example, who told me about Bitcoin right as it was starting. Now he's into cryptocurrencies. He owns NFTs. Heck, he has probably sat with more billionaires in the past few months than I have in my life. He just gravitates toward big business and big people.

I'll never have KJ's natural grace in working the entire room and forming new relationships—but I've learned how to be more outgoing by watching him do it.

Kayla and KJ arrived during the years Dawn and I were married. That marriage did not last, and the subsequent union with my second wife, Gwen, gave me three more special mentors.

Monique came into my life when she was eight years old, as Gwen's daughter from a previous relationship. She is the most focused, patient person I have ever met. And it was she and Kayla who convinced me to get into acting.

She is also in show business—as I write this, she is a regular on the Disney+ series *Big Shot*. She willed herself to that level of success. If Monique has to read twenty pages of a script for an audition, she'll make sure to rehearse twenty-five. If she has to be somewhere at three o'clock, she'll be there at two thirty.

I came across something that Kobe Bryant once said, that he makes contracts with himself and does not break them. That's Monique. If I ask Monique to come over and watch her two youngest siblings tomorrow, she might say that she would love to but can't because she has to go over lines or make a tape of herself at that exact time.

She will have already planned for tomorrow. I never get upset with her about not breaking a contract with herself, because she has never once done it. That's the way she is, and it works for her.

Kayla will break a contract. KJ, he'll break a contract. I certainly do it. If I have an appointment at ten, I might just have to reschedule for one because I forgot about another commitment.

Monique would never do that, and she has been that way since the first day I met her. Many times since, she has used that focus and drive to help me see new possibilities for myself.

A few years ago, a friend of mine who was a producer on the show *Grown-ish*, a sequel to the popular sitcom *Black-ish*, called to offer me a part as myself in one of their episodes. Monique and Kayla taught me how to study for a sitcom part, how to learn the lines and prepare for the shoot. Their focus rubbed off on me, because it seemed to go pretty well.

In 2020, I was offered a part—as a fictional character for the first time—in the Adam Sandler movie *Hustle*. When the opportunity first arose, I was inclined to say no. It was one thing to do a cameo as myself, but I wasn't an actor.

But Monique and Kayla talked me into it, then helped me prepare again. This was really different for me. I don't read lines on TNT; I say what I believe.

In our home, Monique taught me how to integrate a new and

different person into a preexisting pair of siblings and a blended family. Growing up in the melting pot of New York City helped, too, because it exposed me to so many personalities, dialects, religions, everything. That led me to understand that everyone needs the latitude to be themselves.

You can't force everyone into one type of environment or culture. You have to play in a large enough sandbox where everyone can fit. This is like Coach Smith in North Carolina knowing that endless team meetings weren't the way to build cohesion; he approached people as individuals to figure out who they were and what they needed.

In parenting, that means you have to realize that blanket rules for everyone don't typically work. Let's say Monique is studying until two a.m. and KJ has practice first thing in the morning. It wouldn't make sense to give them the same curfew.

The issue of fairness is one that many parents, myself included, have struggled with. Parents compare their approach to each of their children and fall into the trap of thinking that what they did for one, they have to do for another.

But each child's needs are different. One might need you to show up for every game, while another might prefer that you drop them off.

Kayla wanted attention. KJ wanted a ride. When Monique joined our family, she provided a valuable lesson in how to integrate someone with a different approach and personality. She needed space.

Seeing this helped me to avoid comparing or feeling guilty. I don't automatically do for one child what I do for another. I just try to pay attention to their needs.

Monique was the one who helped blend our family. Then Malloy arrived in 2008 as the first child born to me and Gwen. I wanted to name him in a way that would honor my high school coach, the legendary Jack Curran at Archbishop Molloy. "Jack" didn't feel quite right, so Gwen and I came up with Malloy.

It very quickly became clear that he was the most emotionally aware of all of us.

One day, Malloy's third grade teacher approached me. "I just want to thank you for what Malloy did for me," she said.

Apparently, after Malloy gave her the standard "Good morning, how are you?" greeting that morning, and she said, "Fine," he stopped.

"No," he said. "How are you really doing today? Because I can see some stress."

It turns out that she'd had a traumatic day. Malloy's intuition and comment had made her feel much better.

To me, his ability to be in tune was a result of his position as the connector in our family. He was the first person to have a biological relationship with everyone: a brother to Kayla, KJ, and Monique, a son to me and Gwen.

Malloy was the common thread. He is able to connect with everyone in the house. His little sister can annoy the hell out of him, but when they're by themselves in a room, he has a deep empathy for her.

The same applies to everyone, actually: when he's with you, he understands what you're going through and wants to help.

One day at TNT I walked into the makeup room and could tell from the body language of our makeup artist that she was having a bad day.

"Are you all right today?" I asked.

At that, she broke down crying. I hugged her. "No one noticed, Kenny," she said.

Well, I learned that awareness from Malloy.

London was our last, born in 2011. I hate to say this, because I don't like to compare, but she is a quilt stitched from the best pieces of all of us. She is the most athletic. She has the biggest personality, but she can also focus as well as anyone. It's like she took every quality from each of us and became the pinnacle.

It became my job to help her harness the highs. Superman can run through the building, but he's going to leave a bunch of rubble behind him, you know what I mean? She will have the talent and credibility to be whatever she wants, but at a certain point she'll have to streamline the ambition and energy.

I have been around people like her. Michael Jordan, with his intelligence and drive, could have excelled in just about any field, but he pursued basketball. Bill Russell could have been Malcolm X, but he chose to be Bill Russell.

It's not nearly time for London to choose. She has to be a kid first. But I would like to think that I have a unique vantage from seeing all these greats up close—the people I have described in this book—and can help direct her abilities.

That's what all these influences have done for me. Whether it's Michael or Magic or Hakeem, Chuck or Shaq or Coach Smith or Mr. Curran—these people formed my identity.

I want to keep their lessons alive and pass them along to anyone who will listen, but especially my kids. We're living in a challenging time, and we need guidance now more than ever as we try to navigate it all.

I've been lucky enough to live a full life, overcome obstacles, and become a champion in my chosen field.

Kayla, KJ, Monique, London, and Malloy: thank you for helping me get there.

And I can't wait to see what you do next.

ACKNOWLEDGMENTS

I would like to acknowledge the incredible family and friends who have made my life experiences possible.

To my sisters, Wanda and Gwen, and my brother, Vince, you always hold me down.

To my kids, Kayla, Monique, KJ, Malloy, and London, I hope this book serves as a guide to success, exponentially fast.

To Dawn and Gwendolyn, thanks for raising great people.

My crew, Kevin Granger, Jermaine Harris, Segun Oduolowu, Mike "the Barber" Dean, and George Kingland, thanks for always being an ear for my talks and a voice of reason.

Uncle Al Taylor, thanks for being a spiritual guide and friend.

Cousins Cee, Mel, and Co Calloway, there's nothing like those days of our youth.

Joseph, Veronica, and Karen (and the whole crew), stay pushing forward!

My extended family, Raheem Johnson, Fabian Bradbury, Kimani Young, Dain Ervin, Eric Chatfield, and Jay . . . we all we got.

KB—what up!

All my teammates from Carolina, WE R FAMILY.

My Clutch City crew, back-to-back champions, it's amazing how we can go years but when we see each other it's like time never stopped.

The TNT *Inside the NBA* crew . . . you guys make the show that we get credit for!

AIM HIGH till we die! Jet Academy players and coaches, there's nothing like our summers.

On the publishing side, thank you to Andy Martino for helping me put my thoughts together and creating a work I'm proud of.

Thanks to Maury Gostfrand and Doug Johnson for helping to guide my career, and to Esther Newberg for helping with the book idea.

And thanks to my editor, Jason Kaufman, and the whole crew at Doubleday, including Elena Hershey, Milena Brown, and the production department, for guiding me through the process.

And if I didn't get you in this list, read the book—you're probably in it!

ILLUSTRATION CREDITS

Page 1: (top left) Courtesy of the author; (top right) AP Images/ *Newsday*/Kathy Kmonicek; (bottom) AP Images/Wilbur Funches

Page 2: (top left) Jerry Wachter/*Sports Illustrated* via Getty Images; (top right) AP Images/Pat Sullivan; (bottom) AP Images/Walt Zeboski

Page 3: (top) AP Images/Doug Pizac; (bottom left) Bill Baptist/ National Basketball Association via Getty Images; (bottom right) Getty Images

Page 4: (top) Robert Giroux/Getty Images; (middle) Dimitrios Kambouris/WireImage via Getty Images; (bottom) Andrew D. Bernstein/National Basketball Association via Getty Images

Page 5: (top) Kent Smith/National Basketball Association via Getty Images; (middle and bottom) Courtesy of the author

Page 6: (top) Courtesy of the author; (middle) Joe Murphy/National Basketball Association via Getty Images; (bottom) Kevin Winter/ Getty Images

Page 7: Courtesy of the author

Page 8: Courtesy of the author

ABOUT THE AUTHOR

KENNY SMITH is an acclaimed NBA studio analyst for the Emmy Award–winning TNT show *Inside the NBA*. He joins Charles Barkley, Shaquille O'Neal, and Ernie Johnson each week during the NBA season to produce one of the most entertaining studio shows in sports television. He is also a CBS analyst during the NCAA March Madness tournament. Kenny won two NBA World Championships with the Houston Rockets, in 1994 and 1995, and played a total of ten seasons in the NBA. He played his college ball at the University of North Carolina. He lives with his family in California and Atlanta.